Customer Relationship Management

Other titles in the Briefcase Books series include:

To learn more about titles in the Briefcase Books series go to
www.briefcasebooks.com
You'll find the tables of contents, downloadable sample chapters, information about the authors, discussion guides for using these books in training programs, and more.

A
Briefcase
Book

Customer Relationship Management

Kristin Anderson
Carol Kerr

McGraw-Hill

New York Chicago San Francisco Lisbon Madrid
Mexico City Milan New Delhi San Juan
Seoul Singapore Sydney Toronto

McGraw-Hill

A Division of The McGraw·Hill Companies

1 2 3 4 5 6 7 8 9 0 DOC/DOC 0 9 8 7 6 5 4 3 2 1

ISBN 0-07-137954-1

This is a CWL Publishing Enterprises Book, *developed and produced for*
McGraw-Hill by CWL Publishing Enterprises, *John A. Woods, President. For*
more information, contact CWL Publishing Enterprises, 3010 Irvington Way,
Madison, WI 53713-3414, www.cwlpub.com. Robert Magnan served as editor.
For McGraw-Hill, the sponsoring editor is Catherine Dassopoulos and the
publisher is Jeffrey Krames.

Printed and bound by R. R. Donnelley & Sons Company.

This publication is designed to provide accurate and authoritative information in regard to the subject matter covered. It is sold with the understanding
that neither the author nor the publisher is engaged in rendering legal,
accounting, or other professional service. If legal advice or other expert
assistance is required, the services of a competent professional person
should be sought.

> *—From a Declaration of Principles jointly adopted by a Committee*
> *of the American Bar Association and a Committee of Publishers*

McGraw-Hill books are available at special quantity discounts to use as pre-
miums and sale promotions, or for use in corporate training programs. For
more information, please write to the Director of Special Sales, McGraw-Hill,
2 Penn Plaza, New York, NY 10121. Or contact your local bookstore.

 This book is printed on recycled, acid-free paper containing a minimum of 50% recycled de-inked fiber.

Contents

Preface

In one sense, managing customer relationships is as old as the hills. Kristin Anderson's grandfather operated a grain elevator in a small town in Minnesota. Carl T. Anderson knew every farmer by name. These were his customers ... and his neighbors. He knew the names of their families, where they went to church, and whether they or their parents or their parent's parents had immigrated from Norway, Sweden, Germany, or Finland. He knew which farmers would produce the best grain regardless of the weather and which farmers where struggling just to make a go of it. And he knew how important it was to stay connected to all of them.

Carl T. Anderson was a customer relationship manager, though he would never have used that term. For him, CRM wasn't a system or a technology. It was a way of life, a way of living.

It's hard to create that level of customer connection today. Yet, that's just the challenge you face.

Wherever you are in your organization, whatever your title, your success hinges on your ability to be as good at CRM as Carl T. Anderson was ... even better.

"Wait just a minute," you may protest, "my customers are scattered from coast to coast, continent to continent. We do business over the Internet, not over coffee."

That's exactly why we wrote this book. CRM today is about keeping the old-time spirit of customer connection even when you can't shake every hand. CRM today is about using information technology systems to capture and track your customers' needs. And CRM today is about integrating that intelligence into all parts of the organization so everyone knows as much about your customers as Carl T. Anderson knew about his.

Content Highlights

You can journey through these pages cover to cover, or you can skip around, dipping into individual chapters for answers to your most pressing questions about CRM.

Chapters 1 through 3 focus on the concept of CRM. Chapter 1 defines what CRM means in today's business environment and why only organizations with clear and effective CRM strategies are destined for long-term success. Chapter 2 introduces the Customer Service/Sales Profile model, a brand new tool for understanding the dynamic relationship between stand-alone service transactions, repeat customers, and the creation of wonderful customer advocates who love to spread the good word about you and your products and services. In Chapter 3, you'll read about issues dealing with managing service delivery and using the Customer Service/Sales Profile model.

The second portion of the book, chapters 4 through 6, offers practical advice for choosing and implementing a CRM strategy in your own organization. Chapter 4 leads you step by step through the process of defining an effective CRM strategy. Chapter 5 discusses what customer intelligence you should gather and how you might manage it. Then Chapter 6 looks at how you can collect that same CRM data and information.

Next, we look at several special CRM topics. Chapter 7 addresses service-level agreements. Chapter 8 translates CRM into the e-commerce environment. Chapter 9 looks at the powerful potential for CRM to reduce conflict with customers and to help you maintain relationships in those instances where conflict does occur.

The final two chapters focus on sustaining success. In Chapter 10, we show you how to use CRM to avoid the deadly trap of complacency in your customer relationships. And finally, in Chapter 11, you'll learn how to "reset" your CRM strategy and the tactics you choose for implementing it. Committing to this process will keep your CRM approach complete and effective far into the future.

We encourage you to keep a highlighter handy to make plenty of margin notes. Identify where your existing CRM strategy is strong, and where you can make improvements. Capture ideas for building buy-in for CRM, and for sharing information across department lines.

Whether you are a senior executive or a line manager, your understanding of the concepts of CRM and your commitment to using the tools of CRM make a difference.

Special Features

The idea behind the books in the Briefcase Series is to give you practical information written in a friendly person-to-person style. The chapters are short, deal with tactical issues, and include lots of examples. They also feature numerous boxes designed to give you different types of specific information. Here's a description of the boxes you'll find in this book.

These boxes do just what they say: give you tips and tactics for being smart in the way in which to manage customer relationships in different situations.

These boxes provide warnings for where things could go wrong when you're trying to build and sustain customer relationships.

Here you'll find the kind of how-to hints the pros use to make CRM efforts go more smoothly and successfully.

Every subject, including CRM, has its special jargon and terms. These boxes provide definitions of these concepts.

Looking for case studies of how to do things right and what happens when things go wrong? Look for these boxes.

Here you'll find specific procedures and techniques you can use to implement your CRM strategy.

How can you make sure you won't make a mistake when dealing with customers? You can't. But if you see a box like this, it will give you practical advice on how to minimize the possibility.

Acknowledgments

Writing a book is always a collaborative process. We have many people to thank for their generous support. First and foremost, we extend warm appreciation to John Woods of CWL Publishing Enterprises, for his invaluable guidance, patience, and belief in this project and in us. And thanks to Bob Magnan, also with CWL, whose editing skills and encouraging words were both greatly valued. Susan Dees was a terrific source of creative inspiration, always willing to talk through a new idea or concept. Maggie Kaeter was there with priceless support as our deadline approached. Carol's husband, Steven, deserves special credit for his unfaltering support demonstrated in ways too numerous to mention.

We offer a special thank you to our friends at Canyon of the Eagles Nature Park and Lodge—especially Michael J. Scott, who helped us stay true to our target readers—and to the numerous other friends and family members who told us "we know you can do it."

About the Authors

Kristin Anderson is president of Say What? Consulting, a Minneapolis-based firm that works with individuals and organizations to assess existing customer service and communication practices, create and implement change plans, and improve service and communication effectiveness.

Her clients range from *Fortune* 500 corporations to small businesses, from private sector companies to non-profit organizations. Kristin has worked internationally with employees at all levels—from top executives and senior managers, to front-line staff and support area employees.

In addition to writing *Customer Relationship Management* with Carol Kerr, Kristin is author of *Great Customer Service on the Telephone* (AMACOM), and co-author of four books in the bestselling "Knock Your Socks Off Service"® series, including *Delivering Knock Your Socks Off Service.*

Kristin is host of the six-part video training series, "On the Phone ... with Kristin Anderson," created with Mentor Media of Pasadena, CA, and Ron Zemke of Performance Research Associates, Inc. Her articles and interviews have appeared in numerous publications.

An active member of the National Speakers Association, Kristin was honored by the NSA-Minnesota Chapter in 1999 as "Member of the Year." Kristin is also a member of SOCAP (Society for Consumer Affairs Professionals).

When not speaking, training, consulting, or writing, Kristin enjoys on-the-water activities, including racing her MC sailboat during the summer and playing BroomBall during the winter.

Carol Kerr has over a decade of consulting experience, including work as an Organization Effectiveness Consultant for Motorola. She is currently president of *Vision*Research, an organization effectiveness consulting group working with high-tech, hospitality, and public sector organizations. *Vision*Research take a systemic, whole organization view to assessing overall effectiveness, and then works with our clients to close performance gaps.

As a frequent guest lecturer for the Human Resources Development graduate program at the University of Texas at Austin, Carol addresses topics that range from the basics of developing a corporate learning program, to establishing a common understanding of corporate strategy and goals in a global market place, to developing and implementing corporate strategies.

Carol's expertise in how organizations function has allowed her to work with a variety of different types of groups including marketing and sales, product design, manufacturing, facilities, guest services, and even other consulting groups. She regularly finds herself working with clients on strategy development, goal setting, customer service, team building, process improvement, and quality system development.

When not working Carol enjoys camping, cooking, sewing, and auto racing. She is an avid NASCAR Winston Cup fan and regularly attends races at tracks across the country.

Carol has a bachelor's degree in speech communication from North Dakota State University. Carol and Kristin originally met while competing on their respective school's speech teams. She also holds a master's degree in organizational communication from Southwest Texas State University. Carol currently makes her home in Austin, Texas with her husband, Steven and their three cats, Baby, Frisky, and Tigger.

We'd appreciate hearing about your customer relationship management efforts. We can be reached at Kristin@ KristinAnderson.com and CKERR@austin.rr.com.

Customer Relationship Management Is Not an Option

Peter Drucker said, "The purpose of a business is to create customers." Implied in his words and his work is the importance of *keeping* those same customers and of growing the depth of their relationship with you. After all, as research by Frederick Reichhold and Earl Sasser of the Harvard Business School shows, most customers are only profitable in the second year that they do business with you. That's right. Initially, new customers cost you money—money spent on advertising and marketing and money spent learning what they want and teaching them how best to do business with you.

Customer relationship management (CRM) can be the single strongest weapon you have as a manager to ensure that customers become and remain loyal. That's right! CRM is the single strongest weapon you have, even before your people. Sound like heresy? Let us explain what we mean.

Great employees are, and always will be, the backbone of any business. But employee performance can be enhanced or hampered by the strategy you set and by the tools that you give employees to get the job done. Done right, CRM is both a strategy and a tool, a weapon, if you will. In your hands, and in the hands of your employees, CRM comes to life, keeping you and your team on course and able to anticipate the changing landscape of the marketplace. With CRM, loyal customers aren't a happy accident created when an exceptional customer service representative, salesperson or product developer intuits and responds to a customer need. Instead, you have at your fingertips the ultimate advantage—customer intelligence: data turned into information and information turned into acustomer-satisfying action.

Implementing CRM is a nonnegotiable in today's business environment. Whether your customers are internal or external, consumers or businesses, whether they connect with you electronically or face to face, from across the globe or across town, CRM is your ticket to success.

Customer Relationship Management Defined

Customer Relationship Management is a comprehensive approach for creating, maintaining and expanding customer relationships. Let's take a closer look at what this definition implies.

First, consider the word "comprehensive." CRM does not belong just to sales and marketing. It is not the sole responsibility of the customer service group. Nor is it the brainchild of the information technology team. While any one of these areas may be the internal champion for CRM in your organization, in point of fact, CRM must be a way of doing business that touches all areas. When CRM is delegated to one area of an organization, such as IT, customer relationships *will* suffer. Likewise, when an area is left out of CRM planning, the organization puts at risk the very customer relationships it seeks to maintain.

> **Key Term** **CRM** A comprehensive approach for creating, maintaining and expanding customer relationships.

Patients Are Customers, Too

In the early 1990s Midwest Community Hospital (not its real name) recognized that managed care plans dictated where patients went for their first hospitalization. However, it was the quality of caring during their patient experience that determined whether or not individuals and families would choose MCH for their next healthcare need or move heaven and earth to have their managed care plan send them somewhere else. So, a "Guest Relations" program was launched to increase patient satisfaction and loyalty. It involved all patient contact areas, from the security personnel who patrolled the parking ramp, to the nurses and aides, to the facilities management team, to the kitchen and cafeteria staff. It forgot finance. Accounting staff, accustomed to dealing with impersonal policies and government-regulated DRG (diagnostic related groups) payment guidelines, took a clinical and impersonal approach to billing and collections. MCH found that all the good will created during the patient stay could be, and often was, undone when a patient or family member had an encounter with the finance group. MCH learned the hard way that managing the customer relationships extends beyond traditional caregivers, and that to work CRM must involve all areas.

The second key word in our definition is "approach." An approach, according to Webster, is "a way of treating or dealing with something." CRM is a way of thinking about and dealing with customer relationships. We might also use the word *strategy* here because, done well, CRM involves a clear plan. In fact, we believe that your CRM strategy can actually serve as a benchmark for every other strategy in your organization. Any organizational strategy that doesn't serve to create, maintain, or expand relationships with your target customers doesn't serve the organization.

Strategy sets the direction for your organization. And any strategy that gets in the way of customer relationships is going to send the organization in a wrong direction.

You can also consider this from a department or area level. Just as the larger organization has strategies—plans—for shareholder management, logistics, marketing, and the like, your department or area has its own set of strategies for employee retention, productivity, scheduling, and the like. Each of these strategies must support managing customer relationships. Sounds too logical to need to be mentioned. Yet it is all too easy to forget. For example, in times of extremely low unemployment, how tempting is it to keep a less than ideal employee just to have a more comfortable headcount? Or, consider the situation all too familiar to call center environments, where pressure to keep calls short goes head to head with taking the time necessary to create a positive customer experience.

Now, let's look at the words, "creating, maintaining and expanding." CRM is about the entire customer cycle. This is what we'll discuss in Chapter 2 as the Customer Service/ Sales Profile. When you implement your CRM strategy, you will capture and analyze data about your targeted customers and their targeted buying habits. From this wealth of information, you can understand and predict customer behavior. Marketing efforts, armed with this customer intelligence, are more successful at both finding brand new customers and cultivating a deeper share of wallet from current customers. Customer contacts, informed by detailed information about customer preferences, are more satisfying.

Are you a manager whose area doesn't deal with external customers? This part of the definition still applies. First, you and your team support and add value to the individuals in your organization who do come into direct contact with customers. Again and again, the research has proven that external customer satis-

---

MISTAKE PROOFING

CRM Is Strategic

Make a list of the key strategies that drive your area of responsibility. What approach or plan determines your:
- Staffing levels?
- Productivity targets?
- Processes and procedures?
- Reporting?

Now, write down your organization's, or your personal, approach to managing customer relationships. Compare the CRM strategy with the other key strategies. Do they support the manner in which you want to interact with customers? Why or why not?

faction is directly propor-
tional to employee satisfaction. That means that the
quality of support given to
internal customers predicts
the quality of support that
is given to external cus-
tomers. Second, consider
your internal customers as
advocates for your department or area. For you and

External customers
Those outside the organization who buy the goods and
services the organization sells.

Internal customers A way of
defining another group inside the
organization whose work depends on
the work of your group. Therefore,
they are your "customers." It's your
responsibility to deliver what they need
so they can do their jobs properly.

your team, CRM is about growing advocates and finding new
ways to add value.

Finally, what do we mean by "customer relationships" in
today's economy, where we do business with individuals and
organizations whom we may never meet, may never want to meet,
much less know in a person-to-person sense? CRM is about creating the feel of high touch in a high tech environment. Consider the
success of Amazon.com. Both of us are frequent customers and
neither of us has ever spoken to a human being during one of our
service interactions. Yet, we each have a sense of relationship with
Amazon. Why? Because the CRM tools that support Amazon's
customer relationship strategy allow Amazon to:

- Add value to customer transactions by identifying related items with their "customers who bought this book
  also bought" feature, in much the same way that a retail
  clerk might suggest related items to complete a sale.
- Reinforce a sense of relationship by recognizing repeat
  shoppers and targeting them with thank you's ranging
  from thermal coffee cups to one-cent stamps to ease the
  transition to new postal rates.

In short, customers want to do business with organizations
that understand what they want and need. Wherever you are in
your organization, CRM is about managing relationships more
effectively so you can drive down costs while at the same time
increasing the viability of your product and service offerings.

Technology Does Not Equal Strategy

The past several years have witnessed an explosion in CRM tools, especially software applications. According to a recent report from Forrester Research (March 2001), 45% of firms are considering or piloting CRM projects while another 37% have installations under way or completed. These firms will spend tens of millions on CRM applications, often working with ten or more separate vendors.

Yet, the quality of customer service continues to decline. The American Customer Satisfaction Index, compiled by the University of Michigan's Business School, declined an average of 7.9% between 1994 and 2000. At the same time the number of on-line sites where consumers can post their customer service complaints for the entire world to see has risen dramatically.

What's going on here? If CRM is the powerful weapon we say it is, then why isn't service improving?

We believe the problem stems from confusing *technology* with *strategy*. In both large and small-scale efforts, it's not uncommon to see the term CRM used as shorthand for the technology that supports the strategy implementation. As you can see in Figure 1-1, your CRM strategy should drive your organizational structure, which should in turn drive choices around technology implementation. Yet, individuals and organizations become enamored of the technology applications and forget that that they must start with a CRM strategy.

The language confusion doesn't help. Countless articles and reviews of CRM tools and technologies never mention strategy. They imply, or even come right out and say, that the only thing you need to do to have effective CRM is buy the right application. Yes, the right application is critical. But it is your CRM strategy that informs which application will be right for you.

A recent conversation with a new client vividly illustrated this point to us. Steve is the general manager for a new resort located in a remote setting. "What's your approach for customer relationship management?" we asked. "Well, we would like to buy a database management system," he said, naming a particular

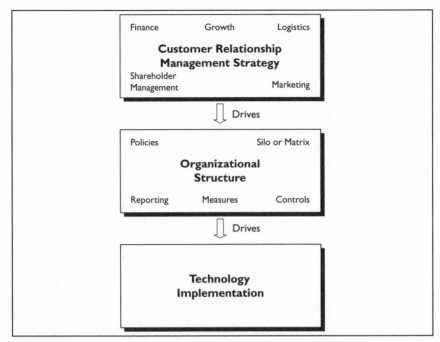

Figure 1-1. CRM strategy drives structure and technology

application, "but right now our revenues just won't support the investment."

We tried again, "What's your strategy for making sure that guests who come to stay one time will want to come back? How do you ensure that every staff member works to create a bond with each guest?" "Well," he began, looking intent, "Everyone just does their best to be friendly and to make the guest feel welcome. We'll do more when we get the database in place."

Steve had fallen into the "CRM is technology" confusion. It's easy to do—and dangerous. Without a strategy to create, maintain, and expand guest relationships, Steve's resort may never have the

> ### Strategy Isn't Technology
>
> Listen to the way the term CRM is used in your organization. Do people confuse strategy and technology? If so, you can be a voice for clarity. Insist that CRM applications and technologies be referred to as CRM tools. Ask how each tool supports your CRM strategy.

revenue to invest in CRM tools—or even to stay in business.

Hotels, at least the good ones, have been managing guest relationships since long before the CRM tools we know today ever existed. So, fortunately for Steve, the seeds of a good CRM strategy were already in place. Front desk employees often asked guests if they were visiting for a special occasion. Information about anniversaries and birthdays was passed on to the restaurant, where complementary champagne or a special cake was provided. Sometimes, housekeeping took part and added special room decorations. However, because Steve was so focused on the high-tech solution he couldn't buy, he wasn't leveraging his hotel staff's natural approach to creating, maintaining and expanding guest relationships. There were a lot of "happy accidents" that resulted in happy guests. But there were even more missed opportunities.

⚠ CAUTION!

Know Your Purpose

Don't get enamored of the tools of CRM before becoming clear about your purpose and what your approach to creating, maintaining, and expanding customer relationships looks like.

Having a customer database is not the same thing as having a CRM strategy. As a friend of ours is fond of saying, "A dictionary is wonderful database of words, but a dictionary can't write a letter for you."

The Power of CRM

The power of CRM comes from the clarity of your approach. Think for a moment about your personal planner and organizer. In a sense, it is your personal CRM tool. What do you use? A calendar with scribbled names, addresses, and a lot of Post-it™ notes? Or are you more organized, using a FranklinCovey™ or DayTimer® binder? Perhaps you are the high tech type, using the latest handheld personal digital assistant (PDA) to keep track of everything.

How well does your personal organizing system work for you?

We'd like to suggest that you can be as powerful with Post-it™ notes as with a Palm®, provided that you are clear about your intention and that you've chosen the right tool for you. We would guess, however, that a fair number of you are using (or at least carrying around) the organizer that someone else thought you should have. Maybe it's even the organizer that *you* thought you should have.

That's what happened to a good friend of ours. "I got a $500 PDA that I've never used, even after the first week of torturously loading in my loose data. I bought it because everybody else had one. They looked so organized and, well, kind of cool beaming things back and forth. I thought, if I get one then I'd look organized too. I'm still carrying it around…along with a calendar and a lot of Post-it™ notes."

Yet, another friend swears by her PDA, conscientiously entering every new name and phone number, religiously consulting its calendar before committing to meetings or projects, even using the portable keyboard to write reports and enter financial data.

> **Know Your Intention**
>
> **Smart Managing**
>
> The more clarity you have about your CRM intention, the greater the likelihood that you will choose the appropriate tools to support it *and* that you will follow through on using them.

A $500 PDA is a bargain if you use it, and an expensive toy if you don't. And the same is true of a $500,000 CRM tool.

To gain clarity about your CRM intention, think for a moment about your own customers, be they internal or external, consumers or business-to-business.

- What drives them to do business with you?
- If you manage an internal support area, ask yourself, given a realistic choice, would your customers choose to do business with you?
- In what ways do you need to enfold your customers in your business, so that

> **Share Your Strategy**
>
> **Tricks of the Trade**
>
> Make sure your team members know what your CRM strategy is and how the tools you've chosen support that strategy. One way is to invite a representative from another area of the organization to a staff meeting to explain how his or her area uses the customer data that your team members collect.

you can better understand what they want and need—
and more effectively provide it?

- What do your customers need and want to have happen
  during their encounters with you?
- What will drive your customers to continue to do business with you?
- What information about your customers will help you
  identify ways you can grow the amount of money they
  spend with you?

The answers to these questions will begin to clarify your
CRM strategy.

Two examples from our consulting experience may help as
you think about your own customers.

Consumer Product Contact Center. Sonjia manages a consumer product call center for a food manufacturing company.
Her group responds to the 800# calls and e-mail requests
offered by product users. Sonjia knows that her customers often
choose these products because these are the brands their moth-
ers and grandmothers used. She also knows that most of them
don't even think about her or her group ... until they have a
product question or concern. In the event there is a problem
with a cake mix, cereal, or other product, the members of
Sonjia's team need to obtain product codes from the customer.
Beyond resolving problems and answering questions, the 800#
call or e-mail contact is a great opportunity to reinforce customer loyalty and gather more information about this new generation of users. Therefore, Sonjia is clear that for her team
CRM has to:

- Create a sense of relationship and reinforce brand loyalty
  with customers who seldom contact the company directly.
- Quickly and effectively turn around a product problem
  or concern.
- Gather product code information so that the potential
  impact of problems and concerns on other customers—
  those who don't make direct contact—can be assessed and
  corrections and improvements can be made.

- Allow customer contact representatives to demonstrate familiarity with an increasingly wide variety of products and packaging options.

Food Brokerage. Maurice owns and operates a food brokerage business, supplying fresh fruits and vegetables to area restaurants. He serves independent restaurants. The chef or souschef places biweekly, and even daily, orders. Chefs by nature aren't hesitant to tell delivery drivers when product quality is lacking. And if they are disappointed, they may well go to another supplier to get the items they want. Disappoint them too many times, and they may make a permanent supplier switch. Therefore, Maurice is clear that to add value CRM has to:

- Profile each restaurant and chef, so that both the brokers who place the bulk food orders and the drivers who make the deliveries know what fruits and vegetables each is likely to order in each season of the year.
- Track satisfaction with delivered merchandise, including refused shipments and those that were grudgingly accepted.
- Anticipate on-the-spot increases in orders, so that drivers can be prepared with extra asparagus, for example, when it looks particularly fresh and appetizing.
- Capture information about upcoming restaurant promotions and special events, in order to predict and accommodate changes.

In Chapter 4, we'll spend more time showing you how to choose the specific CRM strategy that is best for your needs. For now, the point to take away is that the power of CRM lies in the clarity of your purpose. Sonjia and Maurice have clear intentions. How about you?

CRM Success Factors

While clear intention fuels the power of CRM, there are several other success factors to consider. We will focus on five of the most important here. Organizations that implement CRM with a strong return on investment share these characteristics.

1. **Strong internal partnerships around the CRM strategy.** We said earlier that CRM is a way of doing business that touches all areas of your organization. This means that you and your management peers need to form strong internal partnerships around CRM. If you and your organization are early on the road to CRM implementation, now is the time to bring your CRM needs to the table, and to be open to listening to the CRM needs of other areas. You may find that you have requirements that are, at least potentially, in conflict. Resist the temptation to go to war for what you need.

If your organization has gone off the partnership road with CRM, then now is the time to come back together and rebuild partnership with the area that is currently championing CRM. Let them know that you appreciate what they have done. Let them know what data you have to offer and help them understand how you plan to use the data you request from them.

2. **Employees at all levels and all areas accurately collect information for the CRM system.** Employees are most likely to comply appropriately with your CRM system when they understand what information is to be captured and why it is important. They are also more likely to trust and use CRM data when they know how and why it was collected.

Working Together for CRM

At the Consumer Product Call Center, the market research group wanted to add a short customer survey to the end of each customer call. Sonjia worried that both customers and staff would resent spending additional time—customers because it wasn't the purpose of their call and staff because of the pressures to handle a particular number of calls each shift. Engaging in dialogue with her marketing peer about their needs and her concerns helped the CRM team to come up with a workable strategy. Using the power and flexibility of the existing software applications, callers are randomly selected to participate in surveys. Customers are asked if they would be willing to spend an additional few minutes answering three questions in return for a thank-you coupon. Customers who agree are transferred to an automated survey system, while service representatives are freed to respond to the next call.

Getting Everyone on the Same Page

Maurice realized that his sales reps had de facto control of CRM and often felt like they had personal ownership of each customer relationship. In making CRM more comprehensive than a sales tool, Maurice began by thanking his sales team for building strong customer bonds. He shared several stories that illustrated how helpful it was to the sales team when drivers gave them a heads-up about problems or additional customer needs. "Wouldn't it be great to get that kind of information everyday?" he asked, "and not just when you and the delivery driver happen to cross paths?!" The sales team agreed.

3. **CRM tools are customer- and employee-friendly.** CRM tools should be integrated into your systems as seamlessly as possible, making them a natural part of the customer service interaction. A major manufacturer of specialty pet foods redesigned the pop-up screens for its toll-free consumer phone line. In the original design, the final pop-up screen prompted the representative to ask the caller's name and address. Yet, representatives had found that it was easier and felt more natural to ask, "What's your name?" and "Where are you calling from?" and "What's your pet's name?" at the start of the call.

4. **Report out only the data you use, and use the data you report.** Just because your CRM tool can run a report doesn't mean it should. Refer back to your CRM strategy, and then run the data you will actually use. And share that data with your team.

Keeping Guests Happy

Kristin Anderson recalls an overnight at the Duluth, MN, Super 8 Motel. Located near the ship loading and warehousing area, this particular motel lacks any sort of view. Yet, it is regularly booked with guests who are happy to be there. That evening, Kristin observed the front desk clerk poring over a large Rolodex®. Kristin must have looked curious, because the clerk looked up, smiled, and explained, "These are our VIP customers, the salesmen—well, they're mostly men—who come here regularly. I'm just getting familiar with them so I'll recognize them and know their preferences when they check in." This explained the recliner in Kristin's guestroom. "Why, yes. We asked our VIPs what they missed from home when they are on the road. Their recliner was the number-one answer."

Avoiding Customer Ire

Ask your staff if there are any CRM questions that cause customer ire. For example, we've stood behind more than one retail customer who balked at giving the cashier her ZIP code before having her merchandise rung up. In the worst cases, the cashier had no clue why this information was requested, but refused to make the sale without it. In the best cases, the cashier cheerfully and easily explained that this information was used to ensure that stores were conveniently located near core groups of customers, and that she would be happy to ring up the customer's purchases without gathering that information.

5. **Don't go high-tech when low-tech will do.** At Harley-Davidson outside of Milwaukee, WI, during the summer they often leave open the big metal doors to the manufacturing facility to let in any breeze and the cooler evening air. Unfortunately, open doors occasionally let in other things, including skunks. A team met to consider the problem and possible solutions. After discussing the pros and cons of screens, half-doors, or keeping the doors shut, they came upon the ideal solution. When a skunk wanders in, just leave it alone and wait till it wanders back out. Skunks may be Harley fans, but they never stay long.

Organizations that successfully implement CRM look for the simplest solution when implementing their CRM strategy.

A low-tech solution that works for the people who actually use it is more effective than a high tech solution that is cumbersome, costly and apt to be discarded or inconsistently implemented.

The Report Maven

TRICKS OF THE TRADE Make one member of your team the report maven. This individual should learn how to query your CRM database for an ad hoc report to see if you can spot a trend or deepen your understanding of what your customers want or need.

CRM Is Here to Stay

Lee Iacocca said, "The biggest problem facing American business today is that most managers have too much information. It dazzles them, and they don't know what to do with it all."

Keep It Simple

While the hotel chain's corporate office struggled to find a cost-effective way to identify and flag repeat guests by property, one location had already figured it out. When guests were picked up at the airport or greeted by the doorman, a seemingly casual conversation actually probed to see if the guest had stayed at the property before. Then, as the driver, doorman or bellhop passed the customer to the front desk with a "This is Ms. Customer," a gesture that indicated first timer or return guest. Imagine the surprise at the home office when they learned that, for free, the front desk staff was greeting guests with a "We're so happy to have you with us again, Ms. Customer."

Isn't CRM just another management fad that adds to that problem? No. Done right, done well, your CRM strategy sets the agenda for what data you will collect, how that data will be translated into information, customer intelligence, and how that information will be shared across the organization.

We believe that the biggest problem facing business today is that most managers have too much data, and far too little relevant information.

When aggregate customer information is strategically collected and segmented, you can target new customer prospects. When customer preference information is easily accessible, you can craft superior service experiences—be they face-to-face, via telephone, or over the Internet. And when information about changing or additional customer needs is captured, you can expand the depth of the customer relationship.

> **Data** Simply the facts. The fact that you served 40 customers is data.
>
> **Information** Data for which meaning has been interpreted. Knowing that 40 customers is an average number to serve is information.

CRM is the strongest weapon you have to create, maintain, and expand customer relationships and it's here to stay.

Manager's Checklist for Chapter 1

❑ CRM is about managing relationships more effectively so you can drive down costs while at the same time increasing the viability of your product and service offerings.

❑ The strength of CRM lies in the clarity of your approach and purpose. Before taking a single step forward, be absolutely clear about what you want to accomplish.

❑ Remember, customers want to do business with organizations that know them, that understand what they want and need, and that continue to fill those wants and needs. CRM is about making sure you have the information you need to do just that.

❑ Tools enable customer relationship management. Tools don't have to be high-tech. The best tools are the ones that allow you to gather the information you need in the easiest way for both you and your customer.

The Customer Service/Sales Profile

Now you understand that the power of CRM lies in its ability to help you create, maintain, and expand customer relationships. You're excited and ready to begin delving into the process of creating your own CRM strategy, whether at the organization level or as it applies to your specific area or department. Before you do that, we'd like you to take a more in-depth look at who your current customers are and what their relationships with you look like. Our model, the Customer Service/Sales Profile, will help you to do three things.

First, it will show you what kind of customer relationships you're trying to create. Is your success based in initial, stand-alone transactions? Or does the nature of your product or service put customers in partnership with you over longer periods of time? How important is it for you to have satisfied customers acting as word-of-mouth advocates for you in the marketplace?

Second, the Customer Service/Sales Profile will help you identify strengths in your current CRM practices. Even in cases where there's no formal CRM strategy, if you're still in business, you must be doing something right, maybe several or many things. Knowing what right practices have evolved naturally will help you create the greatest possible improvement with the least amount of expense.

Third, because this process creates a visual image of your customer relationships, you will find it helpful in communicating to others throughout the organization. Knowing your current profile and the desired profile will naturally help you focus your energy and attention.

Why Call It the Customer Service/Sales Profile?

We call our model the Customer Service/Sales Profile because every business activity is ultimately justified by how it serves the customer. Even if you and your team never see a cash-paying external customer, the contribution you make must have some positive impact on those external customer relationships or else you should strongly question its value and purpose. We use the phrase "Service/Sales" to remind us of three important truths.

> ### Don't Let the Language Stop You
> Do you work in the public sector or for a non-profit organization? You may want to substitute the word "member" or "citizen" for the word "customer." And if you rely on tax revenue, donations, or grants for your operating capital, you may want to use words like " patronage" or "support" instead of "sales." The point is still the same: you must add value to the individuals and organizations that use your services, buy your products, support you financially.

Truth #1: Sales do not equal relationships. Way back in 1983, Theodore Levitt wrote an article for the *Harvard Business Review* titled "After the Sale Is Over." In it he explained that the sale is just the beginning of the relationship with your customer—a relationship more akin to a marriage than to a one-night stand. And consultants, practitioners, researchers, and authors have been building on this theme ever since.

Yes, the sale is a very important point in customer relationships. However, it is bracketed by the quality of service you are willing to offer, able to deliver, and credited with providing to your customers.

> **Service That Sticks**
>
> Author and consultant Ron Zemke is fond of saying, "Price is a magnet that draws customers in, but service is the Velcro™ that keeps them loyal." Are you "Velcroing" your customers to you by promising, providing, and taking credit for high-quality service?
>
> **Smart Managing**

Truth #2: Service extends beyond the buyer. Whether you're selling in-home plumbing repair or pacemakers or e-business solutions, creating a customer relationship, maintaining that customer relationship, and extending the opportunities you have to do business together mean more than wooing the individual who writes the check or signs the contract. You need to consider all the people who touch or who are touched by your product or service.

Truth #3: Service and sales are on the same team. All too often, we are called into sales organizations or customer service departments that claim that everything would be better if "those other people" in service or sales "would just straighten up and get their act together."

The sales people lament that the customer service people just complain, complain, and complain about pesky details like a few

> **Cultivate the Experience**
>
> The Wild Rumpus Bookstore in Minneapolis, Minnesota, is often listed among the top 10 independent bookstores in the United States. Storeowners know that parents control what their young children read, how much money they can spend on books, and even whether or not they visit Wild Rumpus. Parents are the buyers, yet the experience Wild Rumpus creates for children is the driving force behind its success. Everything about the store—the fish tank behind the bathroom mirror; the hamsters that live below the Plexiglas® floorboards; the live chickens, cats, and reptiles; comfortable chairs for reading—is designed to engage *both* children and their parents.
>
> **For Example**

over-promises or a couple of tight delivery deadlines. "Don't they know that we've got to promise those things to get the sale?"

The customer service people roll their eyes at visions of golf club-swinging sales types teeing off with unrealistic promises and assurances that "the customer service team will be happy to move mountains for you." "Don't they know we have policies? If we did that for this customer, we'd have to make the same exception for every customer."

The truth is that to win the game of business, sales and service have to be playing on the same team. The phrase Service/Sales can serve as a reminder for both groups that you win only when you work together.

The Three Levels of Service/Sales

There are three service/sales levels to the Customer Service/Sales Profile model (Figure 2-1).

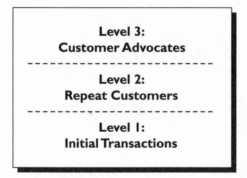

Level 3:
Customer Advocates

Level 2:
Repeat Customers

Level 1:
Initial Transactions

Figure 2-1. The three service/sales levels

Level 1 is initial transactions. At this level you are focused on discrete, initial interactions or stand-alone sales. This is the foundation for every business or organization. Yet, we know that the more money, time, and energy you must invest in getting customers to come to you in the first place, the harder it is to be profitable just working at this level. As we noted in Chapter 1, it's not unusual for customers to actually cost you money the first time they do business with you. Just consider the acquisition costs for your customers (Figure 2-2).

Traditional Cost of Acquisition

$$\text{Cost of Acquisition} = \frac{\text{Cost of Campaign}}{\text{Number of Customers Gained}}$$

For example, a Nature Reserve Center might calculate its COA as:

$$\frac{\text{Print Advertising} + \text{Radio Advertising} + \text{Web Site}}{\text{Number of first-time visitors during campaign}} = \$30 \text{ cost per new customer}$$

Actual Cost of Acquisition

$$\frac{\text{Cost of Campaign} + \text{Cost of Staff Time} + \text{Cost of Service Breakdown}}{\text{Number of Customers Gained - Number of Customers "Lost" During This Time}}$$

$$\frac{\begin{array}{c}\text{Print Advertising} + \text{Radio Advertising} + \text{Web Site} + \\ \text{Staff time to give tours/explanations/answer questions} + \\ \text{Cost to correct service problems and misunderstandings}\end{array}}{\text{Number of first-time visitors - number of customers "lost"}} = \$220 \text{ cost per new customer}$$

Figure 2-2. Traditional versus actual cost of customer acquisition

As you can see, in order for our Nature Retreat Center to be profitable at Level 1, they need to:

- Identify customers at risk of leaving, never to return, and find out how they can woo them back.
- Look for ways to teach new customers more about what the Nature Retreat Center offers and how it works so that there are fewer avoidable service issues.
- Give staff tools and training on ways to turn their interactions into revenue-generating opportunities while at the same time making guests feel well served.

It will be important for the Nature Retreat Center to focus on these improvements. When initial transactions run smoothly, with a minimum of fuss or error, it provides a strong foundation for future business.

Level 2 represents repeat customers. At this level you're focused on getting customers to return for a second, third, or fourth time. Customers may come back for the same purchase— like the loyal Caribou Coffee customer, cordially known by the staff as the "extra large, skim latte with Caribou cookie." Or the

The Door Swings Both Ways

Don't focus on attracting customers and then neglect what it takes to keep them.

A good friend went to a local print shop for her business cards. The owners were active in the neighborhood association, advertised in the local weekly newspaper, and offered lots of deals for " savings on your next purchase. "When she got her first set of cards, she discovered a misprint—one that wasn't in the proof. They apologized and rushed to reprint her cards. Again, there was an error. "After the third time, I wondered if the Keystone Kops were running the presses," she explained. "They so wanted me to come back there for my letterhead and other printing needs, but really!"

We suspect that if they'd put the effort into getting transactions right that they'd put into making neighborhood relationships, they would still have our friend's business.

customer may turn to you for a variety of products and services—like a car insurance customer who comes back to her agent for homeowner's, disability, and life insurance.

Repeat customers develop greater economic and emotional ties with you. And they bring with them an expectation that you will value those ties. For example, the Caribou Coffee customer may expect you to save the last Caribou cookie for him. And the insurance customer will look for a discount for having car, home, and life insurance with the same provider.

Your CRM strategy will tell your team how much importance to place on repeat customers. CRM tools will help your team identify these precious members of your customer mix and prompt team members to notice and value their extended relationship with you.

Reward Repeats

Frequent buyer programs are a great way to offer extra value to repeat customers. The best examples of these make the process easy for both customer and employee.

The top level of the model is customer advocates. Level 3 represents those customers who are not just satisfied and willing to do business with you again. These customers actively tell others about their positive experience. They spread the good word. You might even consider them to be active participants on your marketing team.

As you can see, each level builds upon the level before. Without quality initial transactions, customers won't want to do business with you again. And it's the customer who sees himself or herself in a positive relationship with you who can provide the strongest advocacy for you and your products and services.

> ### Who's Ready to Advocate?
>
> Customer satisfaction surveys often group responses, reporting back that "90% of our customers are satisfied or very satisfied." Both *satisfied* and *very satisfied* customers are likely to do repeat business with you—but only the *very satisfied* are ripe to be customer advocates.
>
> Make sure your customer satisfaction survey reports help you to see the difference.

The Shape of Your Custom Service/Sales Profile

The shape of your Customer Service/Sales Profile reflects the relationship among these three levels. It is driven by the nature of the product or service you offer, the expectations of your customer base, and the forces of market competition.

There are three basic Customer Service/Sales Profiles: the Pyramid, the Hourglass, and the Hexagon.

The Pyramid Profile

The Pyramid (Figure 2-3) is the conventional way to see the relationship among the three levels. It applies to the majority of businesses. Consider a retail department store, such as Minneapolis-based Target Stores. Each day hundreds of customers walk through the doors of any one Target location. Still more customers shop online at Target.com. Those customers represent the base level of initial transactions. The percentage of those customers who are loyal to Target, who regularly seek Target in preference to its competitors, make up level 2. At the top are those customers who actively send their friends, family members, and even business associates to Target. They tell positive stories about staff and service.

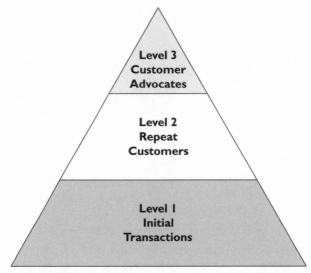

Figure 2-3. This Pyramid is the most traditional profile

As you might imagine, not every pyramid looks like a perfect isosceles triangle. For example, in some business models, there's a very strong emphasis on repeat customers but less on customer advocates. As one salesperson for a large-scale computer application told us, "Yes, I think my customers are happy enough to keep doing business with me. And I'm working very hard to keep them happy. But, no, I wouldn't want to put my existing customers in a room with my prospects."

If you don't trust your repeat customers to help you "sell" a prospect, then you have pyramid with a broad middle and a small top. It might be tempting to tell this sales professional to go out and create more advocates. And that would be a dangerous shift if it meant losing focus on the repeat customer group. In a Pyramid Profile, customer advocates grow directly out of exceptionally well-satisfied repeat customers.

The Hourglass Profile

The Hourglass Profile (Figure 2-4) is less common. In the Hourglass, you have a broad base of initial transactions, only a few of which become repeat customers. However, you seek to

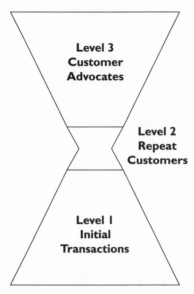

Figure 2-4. The Hourglass Profile is appropriate when the buying cycle is long or when your product or service is a one-time purchase

create customer advocates from as many of those initial transactions as possible.

Consider the relationships between a real-estate agent and her customers. Diane, an agent in the business for over 15 years, explains that she sometimes gets a second sale, but rarely a third from most of her customers. "I get a second sale when the initial house is their 'starter home.' After two or five years, they are ready to move up. Many of my clients are selling because they are moving out of the area. I don't get a second chance with them."

Yet Diane's business is booming. Her company has recognized her as a top performer for several years in a row. "I think my secret is really no secret. My clients are my biggest sales force. They are constantly recommending me to people they know who are buying or selling a home."

An Hourglass is most stable when it has a strong base of initial transactions and those transactions are handled in such a superior way that customers are eager to tell others about their experience. When this happens, the Profile creates its own self-

Smart Managing

Know What Suits Your Shape

If you have a Pyramid Profile, communication with existing customers will focus on *repeat business*, making the next sale.

If you have an Hourglass Profile, communication with existing customers will focus on *recommendations*, getting referred for the next sale.

Both are important, but which is most important to your success— repeats or recommendations?

renewing energy. Diane, for example, does put considerable time and effort into maintaining contact with past clients, sending them calendars and other reminders, and keeping her name and phone number easily accessible so clients who have an inclination to recommend her will find it easy to do so. But Diane is the first to admit that this process works with more ease and flow than in the early years of her business, when she was less sure of herself and less sure about satisfying her clients.

The Hexagon Profile

In the Hexagon Profile (Figure 2-5) describes a business that is very stable. It has all the repeat business it can handle or wants, so it feels little motivation to actively seek for Level 3, customer advocates. It also feels no strong motivation to focus on initial transactions, since there are already plenty of repeat customers

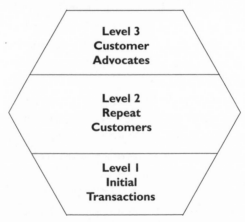

Figure 2-5. Seemingly stable, the Hexagon Profile is actually very vulnerable, lacking a strong base of initial transactions

... for the moment. This is a vulnerable profile. Should anything disrupt the core of repeat customers, the business will be hard-pressed to replace them.

The Hexagon Profile can self-destruct when supply and demand are no longer in balance and no longer working in your favor. We watched a small advertising agency go under because it was operating under this profile. Secure with its three major clients and a steady mix of small "filler" jobs, the team focused on doing the work. They paid little attention to growing their "filler" jobs into something more, or to getting their name out to encourage new clients, or even to inviting their current clients to recommend them. When first one and then two of the core clients moved their business, the team couldn't replace them quickly enough to stay viable. "I haven't done marketing in so long, I don't know where to begin," one owner sighed. How much easier it would have been if they'd asked for letters of recommendation and referrals months before, when their core customers were active and satisfied.

Pitfalls of the Customer Service/Sales Profile

There are two common pitfalls that cause individuals and departments to become misaligned around their Customer Service/Sales Profile.

1. **Focusing on the top.** It's personally and professionally satisfying to have customer advocates. Human nature

---

If You're Out of Steak, Sell the Sizzle

Smart Managing

The natural profile for Harley-Davidson Motorcycles is the Hourglass. Purchasers of the prized bikes quickly become advocates. In fact, they are often so anxious to be part of the Harley-Davidson family that they are advocates even before taking title to their new machine.

When demand for these classic vehicles exceeded supply, the company avoided moving into a complacent Hexagon Profile by creating a special community for bikers-to-be. This involved purchasers in the initial transaction—even though it could take up to two years to receive their product.

Just Ask!

Use customer satisfaction surveys and focus groups to find out both what satisfies and what disappoints your customers. If you aren't getting any complaints, you aren't asking the right questions or the right people.

yearns for that positive affirmation. Beware of taking their praise so much to heart that you begin to think that anyone who isn't an advocate is just too picky and hard to please.

2. **Focusing on the front door.** Initial transactions are critical, but they're only one step in the customer relationship. When a rush of activity comes ... and especially when it stays ... it's easy to get caught up in processing customers through faster and faster—"Don't worry if it's not perfect, someone else is waiting to be served!" Yet, when the rush is over and you're waiting in vain for the next new customer, all those initial transactions will be looking for someone else, someone more service-oriented, for their next transaction.

Don't Treat All Customers the Same

A travel agency owner we know shared a hard lesson he learned during one of the airline fare wars. "Customers were calling night and day, on hold for 30, 40 minutes or more waiting to talk to an agent. And my agents were doggedly working to get to everyone. Most of them were people who'd never called us before and probably won't call us again. And while we were tied up with them, lots of our regular customers got frustrated and mad, and some have left. They felt we owed it to them to serve them first. And, you know, I think they're right."

CRM and Your Profile

So, what's your Customer Service/Sales Profile? Are you operating as a Pyramid? As an Hourglass? Or as a Hexagon? It's important to know what kind of customer relationships you've been creating so that you can be thoughtful and strategic in choosing what kind of customer relationships you want to create from this point forward.

What works about your current profile? And what

would you like to change? The answers to these questions will help to shape your CRM strategy. You will find that it's easier to align your team—and your organization—around a clear and consistent CRM strategy if you all share a common vision of your Customer Service/Sales Profile.

Manager's Checklist for Chapter 2

❏ Where is your customer relationship emphasis? Is it on creating initial or stand-alone transactions (Level 1)? Is it repeat customers (Level 2)? Or do customer advocates (Level 3) drive your success?

❏ You can't have a customer relationship without service and sales working together, creating positive experiences for the customers who give you the money and for everyone else at the customer site who touches or is touched by your product.

❏ The Pyramid Profile is the most common. Initial transactions lead naturally to repeat business and a percentage of those repeat customers move into advocacy.

❏ The Hourglass Profile describes relationships with customers where the buying cycle is long. The focus is on turning customers into advocates based on their initial experience with you.

❏ The Hexagon Profile represents an organization at risk. It may seem stable, but it lacks a strong base of initial transactions and has few customer advocates to help drive new marketing efforts.

Managing Your Customer Service/ Sales Profile

What's your Customer Service/Sales Profile? To determine your profile, look at each of the three levels. What percentage of your customer transactions are initial or stand-alone transactions and what percentage of customer transactions represent repeat business relationships? Next, of your total customer base, what percentage do you consider to be real advocates?

Let's follow our examples from Chapter 1—the consumer product contact center and the food brokerage—to see how the process of managing to your Customer Service/Sales Profile unfolds.

Sonjia's Contact Center

Sonjia is creating a profile for her consumer product contact center (see Chapter 1). When she looks at the customer traffic, she knows that most of contacts are first-time/one-time. A consumer has a product question or concern, receives an answer, and then may not ever have a need to contact the center again. She puts these contacts in Level 1, even though the individual consumers who call or e-mail may be loyal repeat users of the

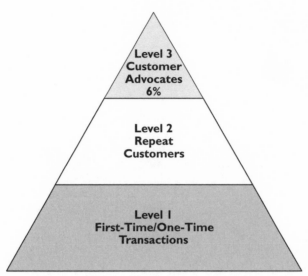

Figure 3-1. Sonjia's consumer product contact center—Pyramid Profile

product. There's a segment of consumers who contact the center repeatedly. Sonjia puts this group in Level 2. Finally, she learned in a recent Customer Satisfaction Survey that about 6% of those who contact the center have positively recommended the center to other customers. Sonjia puts that percentage in Level 3.

As you can see in Figure 3-1, the consumer product contact center has a Pyramid Profile. Using this visual image, Sonjia can begin to lay the groundwork for her CRM strategy. (We'll get into crafting a strategy in Chapter 4.)

First, Sonjia will want to compare this profile with her desired profile.

For example, research suggests that if a consumer complaint or concern is handled quickly and easily in the first contact, there can be an opportunity for an add-on sale. To take full advantage of this, Sonjia might look for ways her CRM strategy could encourage more repeat customers and thus more sales opportunities. This would change the proportions in her ideal Pyramid Profile, reflecting a greater emphasis on repeat customers (Figure 3-2). The percentages for Levels 1 and 2 should equal 100%. These levels represent customer transactions with

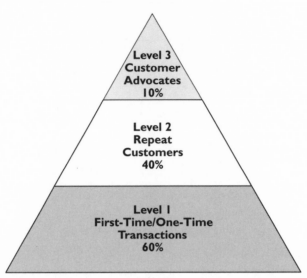

Figure 3-2. Sonjia keeps the Pyramid Profile but increases the emphasis on Repeat Customers, Level 2

you. Level 3 is the percentage of your total customer base who feel so positive about their experience that they actively want to, and do, tell others.

Sonjia may determine instead that repeated contacts mean that a customer's concern or complaint was not handled in the initial contact. In this case, she may be satisfied with her existing profile.

Or, Sonjia may believe that a more ideal profile would be some form of the Hourglass (Figure 3-3), where initial transactions are handled so well that customers don't feel the need to call again, but they speak positively about their experience to others. So, her CRM strategy then would focus on supporting her team in resolving customer contacts right the first time *and* encouraging those customers to share their positive experiences with others.

Next, keeping in mind the profile she wants to

Study Your Shape

Smart Managing What is the shape of your Customer Service/Sales Profile? Is this profile working well for you and your team? Or might you be better served by seeking a different profile?

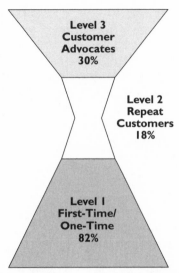

Figure 3-3. An Hourglass Profile reflects greater emphasis on Customer Advocates, Level 3

create, Sonjia can consider how well she and her team currently manage transactions at each level. What are the best practices that allow customer contact representatives to resolve problems during the initial transaction? Are there information technology systems and supports, such as a customer-facing Web page with easily accessible answers to the most frequently asked questions, answers that work well to satisfy customers? What is it that causes 6% of customers to move into the level of advocacy? These are right practices that Sonjia will want to reinforce with her CRM strategy.

Don't Assume All Repeat Customers Are Good

An important issue for a service group like the consumer product contact center is to know if repeated contacts are good or bad. A repeat customer may be someone who's discovered extra value by contacting you—or someone with complaints. It's meaningful to segment your repeat customers. How many contact you with a service problem? How many contact you because they receive value from the contact? This will help you determine whether or not, and how, you want to grow at this level—key information for your CRM strategy.

Finally, Sonjia can look for ways to improve the customer experience by asking these questions:

- What isn't happening that should be happening?
- What is happening that shouldn't be happening?
- What is happening that could happen better?

Evaluating Best Practices

✔ Love It
✔ Lose It
✔ Improve It

Speaker, trainer, and consultant Robin Getman of Minneapolis-based InterACT Group uses these categories when she evaluates best practices. "You can use these categories when you ask customers for feedback or when you are working with your own team to improve service and product quality," explains Robin. What do you need to lose? What should you improve? And what do your customers and your team members just love?

Don't just look at face-to-face and phone-to-phone interactions. Consider, too, how customers experience any self-service features, such as an interactive Web site, and at how the processes, policies, and procedures affect the customer's perception of service and value.

Maurice's Food Brokerage

Looking at the three levels of customer interaction reveals something very important to Maurice. His current Customer Service/Sales Profile is a Hexagon (Figure 3-4). The bulk of his business is in Level 2, repeat business. These are his "steady customers."

Although he's on the lookout for new clients, there are a limited number of restaurants in his community. And, to be frank, many new restaurants just don't make it. So, Maurice is understandably reluctant to extend credit or make deliveries to a new venture that is likely to pay late ... or not at all.

Restaurant owners, and chefs in particular, are an opinionated group, not shy at all about giving "constructive" feedback on product quality, price, and service delivery. Maurice understands, "Margins are very, very tight and it's their reputation on

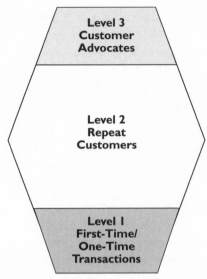

Figure 3-4. Maurice's emphasis is on Level 2, Repeat Customers

the line." Although he's proud of the name he's earned in this marketplace, Maurice hesitates to put many customers in Level 3, advocacy.

We know that the Hexagon Profile can be risky if anything happens to disrupt the "steady customers" at Level 2. However, given the nature of this marketplace and Maurice's years of experience in the business, he believes the Hexagon is the right profile for him. The Hourglass would be an obvious mismatch because it de-emphasizes repeat business, Maurice's bread and butter. And, the Pyramid doesn't work either because, as Maurice might say, "If I'd wanted that many stand-alone trans-actions, I'd go into in the grocery store business."

To keep his profile stable, Maurice will need a CRM strategy that balances emphasis on repeat customers with appropriate attention on initial transactions and nurturing customer advocates.

Now, like Sonjia, Maurice can look at how he and his team manage transactions at each level, looking first at right prac-tices and then at the gaps. Here are examples of what Maurice is likely to see.

Steps Toward Stability

Smart Managing Tightly niched industries and marketplaces where there are a very limited number of potential customers or just a few major players often create Hexagon Profile conditions. There are two creative ways to move to reduce vulnerablity.

Diversify your product and service offerings. How could you creatively apply what you know and what you offer to other markets?

Create scalable workforce solutions. For example, you may want to use more contract or outsource employees so that when your Level 2 business shrinks, you can adjust payroll accordingly.

Right Practices for Repeat Customers

Maurice and his team regularly offer special deals or make special arrangements to assist long-term, high-volume customers. It's something his customers expect—and it's a smart business decision. This is a right practice. Maurice's CRM strategy should reflect the fact that some customers are economically more important and worth more concessions and accommodations.

Drivers create personal relationships with the kitchen staff members who take charge of the delivered goods. Although these individuals often don't place the orders or have the final say on what's acceptable or not acceptable, they can be a powerful internal force, relaying information about product availability and upcoming specials to the chef or restaurant owner. Maurice's CRM strategy and the tools he chooses to support it should support Truth #2, service extends beyond the buyer.

Opportunities to Improve Initial Transactions

All this "special" treatment for Level 2 business could make a

Excellent Explanations

Tricks of the Trade Some people are great with words and know how to say just the right thing in just the right way. Use their skill and expertise to create model "excellent explanations" to share with other employees. Kristin Anderson and Ron Zemke provide many examples and models for this in their book, *Knock Your Socks Off Answers: Solving Customer Nightmares and Soothing Nightmare Customers* (AMACOM Books).

> ## Avoid Making Any Customers Feel Less Important
>
> **⚠ CAUTION!**
>
> Systems can also contribute to that "second-class" feeling. A hospital we know offers cafeteria food at a lower cost to employees and physicians. They consider this special accommodation to these internal customers a good business decision, and we're inclined to agree. The problem? Two systems.
>
> The first is the price signage in the cafeteria area. It lists the discounted price first and the "regular" patient/family member/guest price second, so it seems that external customers are suffering a surcharge at the hospital cafeteria. A simple change in the order of the prices will improve external customer satisfaction.
>
> The second system is the manner for determining the employee discount, figured item by item. If the cafeteria were to switch to a percentage discount, then separate pricing wouldn't be necessary and the special accommodation would no longer be obvious to external customers.
>
> Do you have systems that make some customers feel less important?

first-time customer feel like a second-class citizen. Maurice and his team could lessen this negative feeling—and thereby create a better Level 1 experience—by changing the tone of their communication during initial or stand-alone transactions. This is largely a soft skills issue. Team members at all levels need to know when and how to explain the tiered service levels. Otherwise, in the absence of awareness and training, Level 1 customers could hear, "We don't have any of the good asparagus for you because it all went to the important customers."

Nurturing Customer Advocates

Maurice has never formally asked a customer for a recommendation or even for a response on a customer satisfaction survey. It's time to test his belief that customers in this business seldom, if ever, move to Level 3, advocacy. What's more likely to be true is that advocacy for this customer group will look different than in other industries. Although chefs are unlikely to phone each other and rave, "Oh, you have to try MFB's asparagus," word gets around about which suppliers are best. Someone *is* talking. And that implies that there's a way to discover who's talking,

Smart Managing

Work Against the Numbers

Unhappy customers may tell eight, 15, 20, or even more people about their experience.

Very satisfied customers may talk to five people.

The numbers work against you, given that we tend to share bad news and tell stories about the poor service we've suffered, rather than to pass on a good word. Make sure you treat your advocates—these positive service partners—like gold. That's exactly what they can bring your way!

about whom, when, and where. Finding out is the first step toward nurturing customer advocates.

As these examples show, examining your profile provides you with important information. For the remainder of this chapter, we'll share some additional tips for managing all three levels of customer interaction, whatever your Customer Service/Sales Profile.

Managing Initial or Stand-Alone Transactions

Level 1 is where customer relationships are born. Think of these transactions as auditions. Customers use this contact to form impressions, to make evaluations, and to decide whether or not to do business with you again or speak well of you to others.

There are three keys to managing initial or stand-alone transactions for success.

For Example

How Small Is a Small?

We've noticed a trend at movie theater concession stands and fast food restaurants. The old sizes worked fine for us—"small, medium, and large." But we aren't always sure what to make of choices like "child, small, large, and extra value." Whatever happened to medium or regular-size drinks? Carol asked recently at her local theater. "Oh, that's large," the counter server replied holding up a large cup. "Regular is small now, but if you just say regular, I'd give you the large." Huh? "Unless you really want a small, which is the child size."

Do your customers ever feel caught in an Abbot and Costello routine because you've created a unique vocabulary to describe your product offerings? Keep it simple.

Key #1: Make Systems Simple. The more obvious and intuitive your processes and procedures are for both customers and employees, the easier it will be to create a superior service experience. This is as true for traditional bricks-and-mortar retail stores as it is for innovative Internet applications.

Key #2: Feng Shui the Experience. The transaction should progress in a way that feels natural for both customers and employees. Each step should flow easily from the step before. Answering these three questions is a good way to start:

> **Feng Shui** Translated as "the way of wind and water," the ancient Chinese practice of analyzing the building, environment, people, and time in order to create maximum harmony, health, prosperity, and beauty.
>
> Feng Shui the customer experience by looking at ways to increase ease of access, flow of process, and the aesthetics of the setting.

How can you make it easier for customers to get to you? Think about where customers might search for you, such as through online or printed directories, your location, the signage that tells them they've arrived at your location, and the physical process of entering. For example, a slow-loading Web site and a heavy door atop a long flight of stairs could discourage customers from pursuing initial transactions.

How can you streamline the process of doing business? We noted with interest the recent recommendation that McDonald's offer fewer menu choices. The fast-food giant was a pioneer with combo meals that made customer ordering easier. Unfortunately, that evolved into confusion as McDonald's sought to offer more and more possibilities.

How can you make the service environment friendlier and more inviting? Look with fresh eyes at your service environment. It could be the retail sales floor, your online support site, or the way the service representative looks and acts when on-site with a client. Consider use of space, color, and light. Sit in

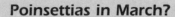

Poinsettias in March?

When you're in an environment every day, it's easy to lose awareness. You no longer notice it—until someone or something brings it to your attention.

Kristin recalls making this point at a hospital in the Midwest. She was interrupted when a woman near the back of the room let out a loud "Oh, my gosh" and started laughing. "I just got it," she explained. "This morning I came here through the front door, not the employee door, because I wanted to see my mom who just had surgery. It's March and there are two dead poinsettias in the entryway, left over from the holidays. I didn't realize until just now—we ask patients to trust us with their lives when we can't even notice when a plant is dead."

Look around your service environment with the eyes of a customer and you too may be amazed at what you see.

the furniture. Stand in line. Log on. Experience it the way your customers do.

Key #3: Capture the Opportunity. Every Level 1 transaction is a customer who may move to Level 2 or 3. You need to capture information that will allow you to invite this customer back for another visit. Without a focus on capturing the opportunity, employees may begin to see customers as replaceable: when one goes away, another comes to fill the space. It's always dangerous to take customers for granted.

Managing for Repeat Business

Level 2 of the profile represents repeat business. This is where most organizations make their greatest profit. If you manage an internal service group or a non-profit organization, this is where you will, traditionally, prove the most value to your stakeholders.

It's helpful to look at managing repeat business from two perspectives. The first is individual customers who make multiple purchases with you over time. This could describe a financial services client purchasing stocks, bonds, and other investment vehicles. Or a loyal retail customer. Or even an employee who turns to technical support for training, problem solving, and new equipment installation.

Key #1: Track the Relationship. Ideally, your CRM database tool should allow you to capture the history of each customer so that you can evaluate and predict purchase and use patterns. Where that's not possible or available, you can still create typical customer use profiles based on customer type and segment.

Key #2: Allow for Variation. Customers want to be catered to. They seldom believe that one size fits all. So create ways for customers to have the experience of customizing. Alvin Toffler wrote about *demassification* as the shift away from the "one size fits all" attitude epitomized in the comment by Henry Ford, "The consumer can have any color he wants, so long as it's black." You can create controlled demassification for your customers. Today's car buyers can have any color they want ... from the palette of colors offered. Where can you give your customers scope to shape their own service experience?

Key #3: Look for Opportunities to Expand the Relationship. Amazon now sells just about everything, including, of course, books. Our favorite Minneapolis restaurant, Tejas, offers its signature salsa by the jar. At Canyon of the Eagles Nature Park and Lodge, they'll recommend a hiking trail and pack you a lunch. What else might your repeat customers want or need? Could it make sense for you to provide it?

> ### Not Just Products, but Services
>
> Staples.com is more than just office supplies. Customers visiting the site will find that "Great service every day in every way!" also means business services, including an "Ask the Experts" site. It's a great way for Staples to keep customers coming back to its site and into its stores.

The second perspective for looking at repeat business is that of individuals and organizations with multiple buying relationships. For example, a bank customer may have checking, savings, and investment accounts as well as a line of credit. Or several or many departments in a corporation may have buying relationships with the same office supply store.

Key #1: Connect the Relationships. A customer with multiple relationships not only represents a greater economic value to you, but also brings additional expectations and assumptions. When your CRM tools capture and connect the relationships, you help your service providers meet the customer's needs and expectations. For example, a corporation may expect and negotiate a volume discount on office supplies based on total purchases across departments, even though some individual departments buy only a few items.

Key #2: Don't Hold One Relationship Hostage to Another. This is often an accounts payable/credit issue. What passed for CRM in not too distant days was often a revised version of the accounting database, since this was often the largest and most accurate source of customer information. However, it was designed to collect money or assess the risk of not collecting money. And it was very conservative in its assessments. We've heard more than one horror story where an overdue bill for some small amount from one small department caused the system to change all deliveries to COD—or worse, putting the entire customer relationship at risk.

Key #3: Calculate the Total Value of the Customer. It's helpful for employees to know the economic value of customers with multiple relationships. You can use real numbers from real customers or you can create value models for typical customers within a segment.

Managing for Customer Advocacy

Level 3 customer transactions are the most elusive. Yes, you can identify customers who are willing to recommend you or who have done so. But you can't *make* customers advocate on your behalf ... or can you?

No, you can't make them do it. However, you can *nurture* and *encourage* them—with powerful results.

Key #1: Know What's Worth Talking About. Customer advocates believe your services and products are worth talking

You Can't Buy Marketing Like This

Saturn recognized the power of customer advocates early on. The new Saturn approach to the car-buying process, and the quality of the car itself, was worth talking about. And customers did! Saturn put some of those same customers in "real people" ads and invited others to write in with their stories. Customers actually competed with each other for a chance to help sell Saturns.

about. So, you need to listen to them to find out what they're saying. Discover what features, what benefits, what aspects of the experience they recount when they recommend you. They may not be the same things you thought most important or most impressive.

What Can You Learn from Customers?

Avon's Skin-So-Soft is more than great lotion. Customers swore by it for years as a bug repellant. Only more recently has Avon shared that claim in its advertising.

Key #2: Changes Worth Talking About. You don't keep customer advocates by doing the same old thing. What was impressive yesterday is ho-hum today. Carol still recalls the first time she visited her healthcare clinic and *didn't* need to present her insurance card—it was all in the computer, printed out and waiting for her. Now she just expects that.

Keep Making Memories

The customers' personal experiences—once so fondly remembered—may fade. To keep those very satisfied customers as advocates, it's helpful to update them on changes and improvements. Keep impressing those customers so they keep promoting you.

Key #3: Prompt Advocates to Share Their Recommendations. Many advocates are willing to recommend you but don't find themselves in conversation with the right people. You can get powerful results just by asking for their recommendations. Here are a few ideas:

Ask satisfied customers for referrals. We know, we know: you covered this in your Sales 101 class. So, do you make a practice

TRICKS OF THE TRADE

Take My Words for It

Customers may be reluctant to write a testimonial simply because they don't believe they're clever with words. Others are just—like many of us—intimidated by the blank page. If you sense this is the case when customers hesitate to provide testimonials, ask if it would be helpful if you got them started. Then, using real customer language, write the testimonial you'd love to receive. Your customer will make changes ... and you'll have a testimonial.

of doing it? It remains an excellent way to build your client base.

Collect and distribute customer testimonials. In your literature, on your Web site, posted on your walls—wherever others may see it.

Give customers anything—from matches to coffee cups to crystal vases—with your name and contact information.

This way your name is easily within reach when the opportunity arises for a customer to recommend you.

Recognize customers who recommend you. At The Sleep Number Store, sales associates ask customers if they know anyone who owns a Select Comfort bed. The associate takes down the name. If the customer buys a bed, the associate searches for the friend in the database and has a thank-you sent out. "I got a check for $50," a friend told us. "You bet I'm going to recommend them again. And I love my bed. Have you tried Select Comfort? You really should ...."

Manager's Checklist for Chapter 3

❏ Create a visual image of your Customer Service/Sales Profile by giving a percentage to each of the three levels: Level 1—initial transactions, Level 2—repeat customers, and Level 3—customer advocates.

❏ Is your profile a Pyramid, an Hourglass, or a Hexagon? Compare the profile you have with the profile that you see as ideal for your customers in this market.

❏ Identify current right practices and opportunities for improvement. Ask these three questions: What isn't happening that should be happening? What is happening that that shouldn't be happening? What is happening that could happen better?

❑ Use the three keys to manage Level 1 initial or stand-alone transactions. Key #1: Make systems simple. Key #2: Feng Shui the experience so it's easy, friendly, and inviting. Key #3: Capture the opportunity to invite this customer back for another visit.

❑ Manage Level 2, repeat business with customers who make multiple purchases. Key #1: Track the relationship. Key #2: Allow for variation. Key #3: Look for opportunities to expand the relationship.

❑ Manage Level 2, repeat business with multiple buying relationships. Key #1: Connect the relationships. Key #2: Don't hold one relationship hostage to another. Key #3: Calculate the total value of the customer.

❑ Manage Level 3, customer advocates. Key #1: Know what's worth talking about. Key #2: What's worth talking about changes. Key #3: Prompt advocates to share their recommendations.

Choosing Your CRM Strategy

M ission statements, visions, strategies ... all have gotten their share of bad press. Do they really do anything to help in the day-to-day business battle? Full of buzzwords and overly general, many are not actually worth the paper on which they're printed. And it's a shame. It's not because writing them, disseminating them, and rallying around them at company meetings takes time that could be more productively spent elsewhere. It's a shame because, to succeed, organizations actually *need* to have a clear mission or vision of where they want to be and a well-defined strategy statement to provide a map for getting there.

As you read Chapter 1, you thought about the approach that your organization and your area take in dealing with customers. You considered your place in your market and what drives customers to do business with you. In Chapter 2, you put that information into your Customer Service/Sales Profile and considered whether the profile you have is the profile you want.

Now, you can build on that and use this chapter to create your own CRM strategy roadmap. We'll take you through the process in detail, so whether you're creating a CRM strategy for

---

Fun with Catbert

Go ahead and let yourself have some fun before you get down to the serious business of writing your CRM strategy statement. Visit Scott Adams' Web site and try the Mission Statement Generator at www.unitedmedia.com/comics/dilbert/career/index.html. If your own CRM strategy sounds at all like something that might appear in a Dilbert cartoon, go back to the drawing board. To stay out of the comic pages:

• Use everyday language. Avoid buzzwords and jargon.
• Make the end goal measurable. By humans. Without spending a quarter of a million dollars.
• Have a workable plan. Strategy is how you get to where you want to be. Just as "Win a million dollars" is a nice thought, but not a workable strategy for personal wealth, "Capture all useful information about every customer who does business with us" may not be a workable strategy for CRM success.

---

your entire organization or just for your corner of its world, you'll feel confident leading the way. And your resulting CRM strategy will help put you and your team ahead of your competition.

CRM Strategy Starting Points

In the ideal world, every organization would have a clearly defined CRM strategy. After all, effectively satisfying customers is the foundation of any organization's success. If you manage in an organization that's fortunate enough to have such a CRM strategy, take a moment to realize how lucky you are. (It's so easy to focus on what organizations fail to provide that it's especially important to give credit and take pride in what they do well.)

If you're not sure what your organization's CRM strategy is, now is the time to find out. Sometimes the issue isn't that the organization lacks a CRM strategy, but that the strategy hasn't been communicated. Find out which area in your company takes ownership for the major CRM tools currently in use. Often, this is the IT or information technology group. Other times it's marketing or sales. Talk with them about the strategy that directed them to use these tools.

Start with Strategy

Smart
Managing

Be aware that the CRM strategy may be rolled into a larger strategy—such as a customer service strategy or even the overall business strategy. You're looking for clear direction on how your organization plans to create, maintain, and expand customer relationships. If that's clear, what it's called is less important than the fact that it exists and that it's working.

A vision that's supposed to drive strategy and states that your company will succeed by "being world-class" is too vague to guide CRM efforts. However, if the vision goes on to detail what "world-class" looks like, feels like, and means to your current and target customers, then you may have what you need to build a winning strategy.

And if no CRM strategy exists? You have two choices. One, you can be the pioneer for creating a CRM strategy for your overall organization. This is a big job, but highly worthwhile and rewarding. Two, you can focus on creating a CRM strategy that's specific to your area or department. If you choose to create a department-specific CRM strategy in the absence of a company-wide one, you need to take extra care to ensure that your strategy supports broad business goals and the efforts of other departments and functions to woo and keep customers.

As we take you through the CRM strategy development process, we'll assume that your organization has an overall CRM strategy and that your goal is to create an appropriate and meaningful sub-strategy for your area or department.

Key
Term

Strategy A large-scale plan for achieving a goal. The term "strategy" has its origins in large-scale military combat planning. In business, think of your CRM strategy as your large-scale plan for achieving the goal of creating, maintaining, and expanding mutually beneficial customer relationships.

Tactics Specific procedures and tools you use to implement your strategy. For CRM they may include your customer database, e-commerce customer interaction tools, your procedures for handling unhappy customers, and customer satisfaction surveys.

Picking the Players

Unless you're a sole proprietor or a very small

business—and sometimes not even then—you won't create your CRM strategy all by yourself. So, the next part of the process is to choose your strategy development team.

You're looking for individuals who:

- Represent front-line customer contact, back-of-the-house support, and management. This can include representatives from all the functional areas that will use the CRM strategy. For a company-wide effort, this might include sales, accounting, and the warehouse, whereas for an internal department, such as an internal help desk, those groups may be extraneous.
- Understand customers and what's important to them.
- Understand the larger business goals and visions or are willing to learn about them.
- Are able to commit time and energy to this process.

Do team members have to understand CRM tools? No. Remember that the strategy informs the tools that you *choose*. You don't need to know how to repair an automobile, or even how to drive, to create a game plan for buying a car. In fact, in our experience, having too many "mechanics" on the team can cause you to focus on the wrong things.

Focus on Participation

Participants who aren't there aren't participating. It's almost always the case that everyone you involve in the CRM strategy development process already has a full-time job. Be sure that you obtain commitment before you begin. As the manager, you can look for ways to ease their job duties in other areas to compensate for the time they're spending on this project.

Preparing for Your First Meeting

Before your initial meeting, it can be helpful to distribute a summary of all the information, strategy statements, and business objectives that you've pulled together in preparation for this effort. A lot of organizations are using a version of the Balanced

> **Key Term** **Balanced Scorecard** An evaluation tool that goes beyond financial measures that organizations can use to assess customer satisfaction, process efficiency and effectiveness, learning, and growth. It was developed by Robert Kaplan and David Norton of the Harvard Business School.

Scorecard to capture and summarize this information along with key success metrics.

If formal data and information about what your customers want and how they experience you is scarce, you may want to conduct one or two customer focus groups or interview a number of key customers before creating your CRM strategy. Internal service providing groups often find themselves in this situation. If you manage such a group, consider conducting a customer satisfaction study before creating your CRM strategy.

Choose a meeting location where your group can have both time and privacy. While we often conduct such meetings on-site, our preference is to use a hotel conference room or other meeting space located away from the normal work environment, to minimize distractions.

Of course, you'll want to have a flip chart available and plenty of wall space on which you can post your flip chart pages. Bring extra markers, masking tape, and push pins (to fasten flip chart pages to the padded walls in hotel conference rooms). And you'll need lots of Post-it™ notes.

> **Tools** **Toys as Tools** Carol Kerr also likes to provide small toys, such as stress balls, Silly Putty™, and Slinkys™, to help participants focus. When individuals who are used to being very active are asked to sit in a meeting for two hours or all day, it's easy to become restless. Playing with a mindless toy during brainstorming actually helps keep everyone on track.

The CRM Strategy Creation Meeting(s)

How long do you meet? How many times? The answers to those questions depend on the nature and complexity of your business. You should expect to spend at least eight hours on this process, possibly

more. Schedule your meet-
ings in four-hour blocks.
Trying to do this process in
shorter time periods can be
frustrating—just when you
get the momentum going,
it's time to end the meeting.

**How Long Will
It Take?**

*Smart
Managing*

As a rule of thumb, creating
your CRM strategy warrants about the
same amount of time that you spent
creating your business plan.

In our experience, 8 to 12 or 1 to 5 just works.

Open the initial meeting with an overview of the information
you sent out to the participants. Thank them for participating,
reconfirm their commitment (whether it's to participate in a single meeting or to remain involved during a series of sessions),
and review the final goal for your work together.

Identify Potential Strategies

We suggest "silent brainstorming" as the first activity to collect
clues about what's important to managing customer relationships. This technique is an effective way to elicit the wisdom of
the group. To begin, distribute pads of Post-it™ notes to each
participant. Ask them to silently and individually create as
many individual notes as they can, listing every way you might
be able to expand, enhance, or improve customer relationships.
Allow 15 to 20 minutes for this activity.

When the participants have finished creating their
notes, it's time to share
them with the group. We
find it helpful to go around
the room and have each
participant read one note,
repeating the cycle until all
the notes are shared.
Encourage participants to
create additional notes as
ideas occur to them. While

**What About Diverse
Customer
Segments?**

*Smart
Managing*

Using the 80/20 rule, it's appropriate to
focus on the customer segment that's
most important to you. If you have two
or more equally important—and different—customer segments, conduct a
separate brainstorming session for each.

this may feel time-consuming, it serves to spark additional ideas
and to ensure that everyone on the team is on the same page.

Now, take the notes and post them on the wall. You will need a lot of space for this because your goal is to cluster the notes into related groups. We get the group going with these instructions:

> First, we're going to place all of these notes up on the wall. It doesn't matter where, so long as they are at a height that can be read and reached by other members of the team.

Wait until all the notes are on the wall before moving to the next instruction.

> Now, our goal is to sort the notes so that similar items and related ideas are together. Again, we are going to do this *silently*. If you disagree about where an idea belongs, you can move it back and forth. If it moves back and forth more than three times, make an additional note so the idea is posted in both locations—but no discussion or argument as you do this.

Depending on the size of the group and the number of ideas, divide the team into groups of two or three people each. Assign one or more clusters of notes to each group. Here's what we tell the participants:

TRICKS OF THE TRADE

Deal with How They Feel

It's not uncommon for the silent brainstorming activity to be met with trepidation or giggles. It isn't what most of us do day to day—and participants may worry that they're not doing it right or just think it's silly. Acknowledge those feelings and fears as you reinforce the importance of the exercise and ask them to trust the process.

> Now take your cluster of notes (or each cluster in turn) and look again at the ideas and items in it. You may notice that most of the things we've written down are actually tactics for serving customers. These tactics cluster together because they are related by strategy—they are part of a common focus. Your job now is to name that strategy.

An average team will need 30 to 45 minutes per cluster for this process.

After the groups have named their clusters, it is time for a report-out. Tell each group, "Read the ideas in your cluster and then tell us what strategy

> **Never Toss an Idea**
> Be sure to keep the silent brainstorming Post-it™ notes, sorted by their clusters. While not every brainstormed tactic can or should be implemented, when you're ready to act on your CRM strategy you'll be glad to have these ideas.
>
> **Smart Managing**

you believe these tactics represent." Create a list of these strategies on your flip chart.

Note: if you're creating your CRM strategy over several meetings, this is a good place to end your first one.

CRM Strategy Selection

At this point, the CRM strategy development process can feel overwhelming. You have so many great ideas, so many directions in which you could go. How can you narrow them down and choose the right strategy?

This next part of the process is about creating *strategy selection criteria* and then evaluating potential strategies using a criteria matrix. You may well have done this before in another context, such as in a formal business plan development process or informally while sorting in your mind your criteria for buying a car or a house. If so, the process will feel familiar. If this is new to you, we invite you to consider all the other times that it might be helpful for you in narrowing options and making wise selections.

To create selection criteria, you will again use brainstorming, but this time everyone is invited to talk. Tell the group, "Building on the work we've already done to identify potential CRM strategies, our task now is to brainstorm a list of all the objectives we have for CRM." This is a good time to revisit your Customer Service/Sales Profile—is your objective to create more Level 1, initial or stand-alone transactions or is it to create more Level 3, customer advocates?

Although most of us are familiar with the traditional brainstorming process, it pays to review the rules:

Brainstorming

Smart Managing The purpose of brainstorming is to get as many ideas as possible out on the table in a short time. Ideas should not be debated or discussed. Remind participants that a negative sigh or look can be as stifling to the brainstorming process as saying, "That couldn't work" or "That's a dumb idea."

Flip Chart Protocol

TOOLS Remind the flip chart scribe to capture ideas using the same words as the person who stated the idea. It's tempting to edit—and all too easy to inadvertently miss or change the participant's intended idea.

When ideas are coming fast and furious, it's helpful to have two flip charts and two scribes. They can take turn capturing ideas.

- Every idea is welcome. Evaluation of ideas should be put on hold until after the brainstorming process is complete.
- Speak one at a time, so everyone can be heard.
- Capture every idea on the flip chart.
- Building on the ideas of others is allowed and encouraged.

Continue brainstorming until the group has run out of ideas. You can usually expect to spend about 20 minutes brainstorming.

Similar to what was done with the cluster analysis, you will now combine related objectives. These are the criteria for strategy selection. It's been our experience that with some groups these items will easily cluster into a handful of five criteria. In other cases, it's a more laborious process that results in a list of 15 or more criteria. There is no right number; however, you'll probably find it best to focus on your top five criteria.

How do you know which criteria are most important? That's a good question. If you have just a handful, it can be easy to simply rank-order them. If you have a longer list, you may want to start by sorting into three categories—must have, nice to have, and not really important after all.

With your prioritized criteria list, you are ready to create a criteria matrix. List each criterion along the top of the grid and

Green Dot, Red Dot
To prioritize five to 10 items, list them on a flip chart, leaving ample space to the left of each and between items. Give participants colored adhesive dots—one green, one yellow, and one red. Ask participants to each silently identify their number-one choice, their number-two choice, and their last choice. Then, have them all go together to the flip chart and place the green dot by their first choice, the yellow dot by their second choice, and the red dot by their last choice. Stand back and let the colors show you which items are most or least important.

list your potential strategies down the left side. Now, looking at each potential CRM strategy in turn, find out how many of your criteria it meets.

Figure 4-1 shows a sample criteria matrix. Your criteria matrix should look something like this. As you can see, Strategy 3 meets all five criteria. Strategy 5, which meets four of the criteria, could also be included in your final CRM strategy.

	Criterion 1	Criterion 2	Criterion 3	Criterion 4	Criterion 5
Strategy 1	✔				✔
Strategy 2		✔			
Strategy 3	✔	✔	✔	✔	✔
Strategy 4	✔			✔	
Strategy 5	✔	✔		✔	✔
Strategy 6		✔	✔		

Figure 4-1. Sample criteria matrix

Your objective is to narrow down your items to no more than three to five key strategies. Taken together, these *are* your CRM strategy.

Your final task in the development process is to write the CRM strategy statement. Unless you have a group particularly talented at this, a draft of the strategy is best written by either the manager or one or two people selected by the team after the meeting. Then a draft can be sent to the team members for review before

One Company's CRM-Driven Strategy

One of our clients, a resort, has developed the following mission, service strategy, and CRM strategies:

Mission: To create an innovative and unique experience for families, groups, and individuals in this fun, relaxed environment, through entertaining, educational programs from a knowledgeable staff interested in making every experience a happy, treasured one.

Service Strategy: We are Hill Country friends creating treasured memories for the naturally curious.

CRM Strategies:
- We will create relationships by understanding the unique expectations of each of our guests and equipping our staff to meet those expectations.
- We will maintain relationships by constantly identifying opportunities to enhance our guests' experience and further our mission, including partnering with other local attractions.
- We will expand relationships by rewarding customers who help us grow our business by recommending our resort to new customers and visiting us frequently.

settling on a final version. The strategy should capture the ideas of the team into a document that provides clear direction for effectively interacting with and serving customers.

Manager's Checklist for Chapter 4

❏ A well-defined CRM strategy statement is your roadmap for CRM success.

❏ A good strategy uses everyday language, supports measurable goals, and includes a workable plan.

❏ Look before you create. Does your organization already have a CRM strategy?

❏ Include on your development team representatives from all the functional areas affected by your CRM strategy.

❏ You can facilitate the development process by:
- Brainstorming potential strategies
- Developing selection criteria
- Applying a criteria matrix

Managing and Sharing Customer Data

The businessperson of just a couple decades ago had to spend a great deal of time and money on intensive research and outdated databases to get even a slight understanding of his or her customers. Today, however, you easily can find yourself overwhelmed with customer information. Current "canned" data reporting on the psychographics and demographics of specific geographical areas is available inexpensively from hundreds of sources. And you can even purchase fairly sophisticated data collection software tailored for your business for just a few thousand dollars.

As a result, the problem more and more is not how to get the information you need but how to determine what you need and ensure you don't get mired in the information swamp.

Return to Your Strategies

Your overall business and CRM strategies will drive your need for customer knowledge. For example:

> ### What Matters to You?
>
> **Smart Managing** "Not everything that counts can be counted; not everything that can be counted counts," said Albert Einstein. Post this quotation near your desk as a reminder while you work through this chapter. As the Chinese proverb says, "Just because you can do something, doesn't mean that you should do it." Don't waste time, money, and resources on data you don't need and won't use.

- If you're a florist trying to boost your wedding business, you'll want to know the age of your current customers, how far they travel to do business with you, how they view your service and product quality, and what factors they consider when selecting wedding flowers.

- If you own a small bookstore whose sales have been dropping the last two years, you might want to know *why* customers stop doing business with you as well as the demographics of your current customer base as compared with that of two years ago. You also might want to know how your sales have changed, especially as the changes relate to the customer base. This is data you can turn into valuable information. For example, you may find that your customer base is now predominantly 50 or over, while your books and magazines appeal primarily to the young.

- If you're a major electronics manufacturer who's looking to boost overseas business, a good place to start is with your current foreign markets. What do they see as your strengths and weaknesses?

In each of these cases, there are multitudes of data available that you don't need. Collecting it could get in the way of your analysis. You need to be able to easily focus your data and information on your CRM strategy. For example:

- As a florist, you know that your customers buy the most roses in May and the most potted plants in June. Nice information if you're trying to increase business in May and June in those two product lines, but fairly worthless for your wedding market strategy.

- As the bookstore owner, you easily can find out which customers prefer romance novels and which prefer science fiction, but that information alone doesn't help much if your goal is to bring in new customers. But compare your current customers with the demographics of your neighborhood and you might find a unique market niche, though.
- The electronics manufacturer may discover that business is booming on the Pacific Rim. Good news, but it doesn't say much without knowing why it's booming. It could be an overall industry trend that doesn't signal any unique strengths for this particular business in this market.

> **Demographics** Statistics such as age, income, and education level used to describe a group of people defined by geography, customer base, or other means.
>
> **Psychographics** Common values and "thought patterns" within a group of people. It's frequently used as a subset of demographic information— for example, urban women in households earning less than $50,000 per year, aged 35 to 45, who believe full-time daycare is bad for children.

Data vs. Information

Once your strategy is in place and you know what you need to find out about your customers, you'll divide the search into two distinct areas: *data* and *information*. Both provide a great deal of knowledge about your customers and, to be most effective, they should be used together.

Beware the Data Dump

Data includes everything that can have a number attached to it. For that reason, it's invaluable in helping you spot major trends in your business. Compare it with data from last year, last month, or even a decade ago and you will find trends that could point to major changes in your business. More young families moving into your neighborhood? If you're a small retailer, that fact alone can dramatically affect your product mix and your marketing strategies.

Typical data are:

- Income
- Years as a customer
- Average purchase
- Education level
- Age
- Number of children at home
- ZIP code or telephone prefix

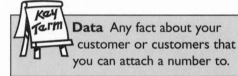

Data Any fact about your customer or customers that you can attach a number to.

In the search for knowledge about your customer, data is the most common place to get overwhelmed. This is in part because data is relatively easy to get. Many government and for-profit organizations collect information about people in specific geographic areas; customers are fairly willing to provide basic information about themselves in a simple survey. Consequently, the danger is that you'll be lured into a sense of satisfaction because you have a lot of numbers that describe your customers when, in fact, you have very little on which to

When You Assume ....

Witness what happened when a one-store clothing retailer in a large urban suburb used data about cars and vacation homes to build a marketing plan for her clothing store:

"These people must make a lot of money, so I'll start carrying top-end items. They also spend a lot of time on vacation, so I'll carry more sportswear," she reasoned. "And I'll support it with a big advertising campaign in the upscale city magazine, which they all must read."

The assumptions made perfect sense. So why did this retailer find her business in Chapter 10 just two years later? Because she didn't realize (as a major competitor did) that her customers preferred to do their sportswear shopping in the towns near their vacation homes and they could afford all these big-ticket luxuries because they were frugal when it came to items such as clothing.

If only she had asked, "How do they afford these things?" instead of making assumptions.

base a decision. "Wow," you say, "70% of my customers own three cars and a vacation home!" Fun stuff to know, but it doesn't

According to Sherlock
"There is nothing so deceptive as an obvious fact."—Sir Arthur Conan Doyle

Smart Managing

do much good unless you know what you're going to do with it. You need to turn your *data* into *information*.

Finding Meaning in Information

What you often need to complement the customer data is information. This is the knowledge that comes from asking questions such as *why* and *how*. For example:

Database A storage place for data that allows you to quickly reference the needed numbers and often allows you to pull out subsets from those numbers. It's often computerized but it can be as simple as an organized filing cabinet. It usually does not store information.

Key Term

- Why do 20% of your customers travel past two of your competitors to do business with you?
- Why did your customer decide to buy the less expensive product?
- How does your customer view your customer service and how important is that to him or her?

Information about your customer can help you make major decisions about reorganizing your business, service offerings, marketing, and other strategies. It can tell you exactly what one customer wants and needs or provide an aggregate view of your customers' feelings about a specific area of your business. It will support trends you dis-

Information Answers received when you ask a customer *why* or *how*. Information makes data meaningful.

Key Term

cover by looking at the data. And it can sometimes show that a trend really doesn't exist, despite the numbers.

Whereas data can be easy to procure, information can be very elusive, time-consuming to obtain, and expensive. There are no CD-ROMs available to describe what your customers feel and how they make their individual purchase decisions. There are no quick questions that can be answered by checking a box or filling in a little circle.

You can procure basic customer information from surveys you put together yourself. However, you run the risk of asking the wrong questions or asking questions in a way that elicits the wrong answers. If the answers are key to your business and accuracy is a must, turn to a professional research firm. They will know how to conduct statistically significant samplings of customers that represent specific demographics, put together a tested survey, have professional surveyors ask the questions, and professionally analyze the answers.

Managing Customer Information—Databases

You know what data and information you need. But before you choose a database system, the place and manner in which you

Dig with Why and How

Jim Meyer owned a small company that made industrial magnets. He wanted to know why three of his major customers moved their business to competitors last year. So, he called up each of his former business clients and asked what the problem was. The answer, in all three cases, was "Your prices are too high."

Jim was dejected. He knew his prices were a little higher but he also knew his quality was better. He didn't want to lower quality to be competitive.

However, he also made a solid decision. Instead of acting on this information, he asked to meet with each of the customers to delve further into the problem. It turned out that the prices weren't really the issue at all. The companies needed better service, such as on-line ordering, just-in-time delivery, and customized specs. Because Jim didn't offer these things, the time and work it took made doing business with him too expensive. His customers weren't getting the value they needed.

Lucky for Jim he thought to ask *why* and *how* his prices were too high. He was able to offer the services the customers needed and regain his business within a couple months.

will store your data, and before you conduct a survey or ferret out the necessary demographic information on your customers, you'll need to make a number of decisions about how you will manage the data once you get it. Among the most important decisions:

What Do You Need to Know?

Use this formula to determine your data and information needs:
- What do you want to know about your customers?
- What data will point you in the right direction?

With the data in hand, ask *why* these numbers are what they are. That will determine what information you need to gather.

- Who will be responsible for allowing access to the database, for deciding what's on it, and for generating reports?
- How much will you tell your employees about how the information will be used?
- How will you share the information throughout the company?

- How will you ensure you're using the information

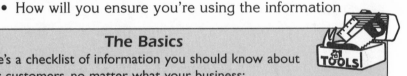

The Basics

Here's a checklist of information you should know about your customers, no matter what your business:
- How long have they done business with you?
- What do they like most about your company?
- What do they feel you could improve upon?
- How often do they repeat purchase? (How does this compare with the industry norm?)
- What life events influence their business with you? E.g., marriage, retirement, business merger, Internet access ....
- Which of your competitors do they also do business with?
- What factors influence their purchase decisions? E.g., product quality, price, delivery options, product line breadth, customer service, speed of purchase, long-term relationship ....
- What is the typical life cycle for each of your products and customers? (This tells you when the customer will be ready to buy again.)

ethically and legally?

- How detailed will the information in the database be?
- What might the information be used for, beyond your primary CRM strategy?

The Employee Connection

Front-line employees are a key connection for managing customer information because they frequently collect it. Whether they're retail sales clerks or highly trained technical salespeople, they're your customer interface. As a result, you must decide what the employees need to know to make their data collection easier.

There's a caution here. It's possible to jeopardize your business strategy by putting the details into too many hands. Your front-line employees don't want or need all the details of your customer relationship strategy. What they do need is a reasonable explanation that will answer their questions and satisfy their curiosity, so they'll be motivated to gather the information. And they need a reasonable explanation they can give to curious customers, so they can motivate your customers to provide the information.

Several years ago a large retail organization wanted to know its customers' phone numbers so it could determine what geographic area they were coming from. This data, they reasoned, could help them focus their marketing efforts more tightly. In point of fact, they didn't need the whole phone number—just the prefix would have sufficed—but someone thought it might do some good down the line to have all those phone numbers.

That was a problem, though. (Remember that Chinese proverb.) When the checkout clerks asked customers for their phone numbers, the customers balked at the idea of giving a retailer such personal information. In fact, many of the sales clerks thought the question was intrusive, too. As a result, the employees soon learned to stop asking. Instead, they simply made up phone numbers to satisfy their quota for the day.

The result? Suspicious customers, annoyed checkout clerks,

Prepare—and Don't Push

When training employees to gather customer data, here are some tips:

1. Tell them why the information is needed.
2. Give them specific responses to possible customer questions about the request.
3. Tell them what to do if the customer doesn't want to give the information.
4. Do not insist that they get whatever piece of data you are seeking from every customer. The reality is that not every customer is willing to participate—and that's important data to capture, too. Plus, if you insist on capturing data for every customer, you should expect a percentage of that data to be "bad," made up to fill in the form.

---

and totally worthless data.

The problem could have been remedied up front by first determining exactly what information was needed, then conducting some very simple training for the checkout clerks.

A relatively small amount of work up front can save countless customer relationships, limit ill will among the employees toward management, and, most important, yield the necessary information.

Try It Out

If you don't know what to tell front-line employees about handling requests for data from customers, pick two or three and give them as much background as they ask for about the program. Then have them work for a day at their jobs, gathering the information from customers. They can then tell you exactly what their coworkers need to know.

To Share or Not to Share?

Customer information is your edge in the customer relationship. As an organization, you want as much information as you can get about each customer because it gives you a better idea how to service him or her. However, when you're dealing with complex, highly profitable relationships, the salespeople have very real issues about the information you might be requesting: too much information shared among others in the sales force could result in internal sabotage.

Sowing Seeds of Discontent

Jim Nelson was a stockbroker for a major East Coast firm. He had worked two years to help design a program for a large multinational corporation. In the process, being a good employee, he shared every piece of information he gleaned from every customer contact. The result? A coworker in the annuities department recognized an opportunity and sold the client on a different product. Jim lost $300,000 in commission—and all respect for his employer.

The company could have prevented this either by asking its salespeople to give only specific data or by screening access to the sensitive portions of the database.

The key to ensuring this doesn't happen is recognizing that the salesperson's contact with the customer is important. Whether they're high-end retail transactions or more complex business-to-business relationships, the company will only lose if it doesn't respect the salesperson-client relationship.

To Hoard or to Share?

Smart Managing Rule of thumb: The less money a salesperson stands to make from a client relationship, the more information he or she will be willing to share with coworkers.

At the same time, your salespeople may like to hoard their data because they have unfounded fears of internal sabotage. In this case, the answer is to go back to your strategy and determine exactly what information you need. Explain to the salespeople why you need the information and what exactly will be done with it. Then collect no more and no less from them.

Beware of Spies

If the information is available to your employees, assume it's also available to your competitors. (Yes, corporate espionage is a reality!) The only way to ensure that highly sensitive data doesn't get into your competitors' hands is to limit its exposure.

Details, Details, Details

Even the simplest customer database can store a multitude of data about your customers. That's great if you know what to glean from the file, but it also can become confus-

**Questions to Ask When Deciding
How Much to Share**

• Is this information that could be obtained in another way, such as through surveys or demographic databases?
• Is this information that a new sales representative would readily get on his or her first couple of calls to a client?
• Is this information that could be used by a competitor—either internal or external—to make an immediate sale?

If you answer yes to these questions, the information can be shared. It's not unique to the customer/salesperson relationship, customers offer it freely, and failing to assess and use it could leave you vulnerable to your competition. If you answer no, it's time to rethink your strategy, possibly asking the salespeople what they feel comfortable sharing.

ing for the people using the database on a daily basis.

The goal is to find the right level of information that makes your operation efficient but also ensures that the customer feels comfortable dealing with you. The second the customer feels you're invading his or her privacy is the second you drive a wedge into your relationship. That will vary for every company, every customer, and sometimes for every transaction.

For example, a medical supply firm may know intimate details about its customers' health and that's

Get a Gatekeeper

Designate one management employee as the gatekeeper for the CRM database. He or she will determine what information is put into the database and what information is available to other employees. This person also should be responsible for ensuring that data is used only for the purpose given to customers when the data is collected.

fine because the customers want that knowledge available to the customer contact people so the transactions are efficient. That same information at the fingertips of a telephone receptionist at the local health clinic becomes disconcerting.

When deciding what information will be available to all employees with customer contact, divide the information in your customer database into three types. Breakdowns for a retail operation might be:

Don't Show What You Know

The way you use your database can provide opportunities to jeopardize the customer relationship.

A large catalog company decided to tie all its information about its customers into its customer service network. When a customer would call, the computer would display the information before the customer service employee even answered the phone.

The customer service workers soon discovered they could take advantage of this information and boost their per-call sales records. "I see you have purchased children's clothing in the past, Mrs. Jones. Are your children in need of new winter coats? We have a good deal on them today."

Instead of making the purchases, though, the customers started to feel uncomfortable that this unidentified person knew so much about them. Sales overall declined and customer satisfaction with the customer service department plummeted.

Important to Know
- Correct spelling of customer's name
- Customer's address and phone number
- Correct pronunciation of customer's name
- What honorific to use (Mr., Ms., Miss, Mrs., or Dr.)

Nice to Know
- How the customer has paid for merchandise in the past
- How long the person has been a customer
- If more than one person from the business or household places orders
- What the customer usually purchases
- What the customer purchased last
- If the customer has had complaints and what they were

Not for General Knowledge
- The customer's age
- The customer's income level
- The customer's marital status and number of children
- The customer's education level
- Answers to specific survey questions designed to discover attitudes about the company and its products and services

Use these levels as a guide for providing access to the information. The first level can be available immediately. The second might come up on the computer screen only after the customer service worker requests more information. The third can be easily screened so it's available only to management.

Data Mining Today and Tomorrow

Even when you carefully craft data and information collection efforts to match your CRM strategy and your overall business strategy, you may find yourself with more numbers than you could possibly digest in a lifetime of customer analysis. However, with just a few legal and ethical caveats, you can use this information for many purposes that can help you spot trends within your customer base. Here are some tactics to try:

- *Analyze the data against last year, three years ago, and five years ago.* Even if you're looking at aggregate numbers such as total customer interactions, differences of more than 5% could signal a trend.
- *Cross-reference the information.* Simple computer programs can take two sets of data and combine them. In that way, you can find out if your customers between 30 and 40 years old spend the most money while those 50 to 60 spend the least, for example. Nice to know for targeting prospects and planning your product line.
- *Pinpoint major problems.* Information retrieved through surveys can point you to major problems you hadn't realized. For example, if you're wondering why no one is using your new online ordering system, customers may tell you that they don't own computers, that it's too confusing, or that they simply like the sound of a human voice.
- *Compare the customer data to your business data.* Did your customer demographics change at the same time your sales in one product line soared? You may have discovered a new psycho graphic component to your customer base.
- *Monitor seasonal changes in the data.* Look for sales

CAUTION!

Follow the Rules

As you use the data and information you've gathered, remember a few rules of the statistics game:

1. *Information is always old.* It can only tell you what your customers did or thought yesterday. It will not guarantee a thing about what they will do tomorrow.

2. *One person doesn't represent the group.* Focus groups and surveys can be a lot of fun because you really get to know an individual's or small group's feelings. However, the only data that can show trends comes from statistically significant samples of the larger group.

3. *Data is not a crutch; it's just a tool.* When Coke introduced New Coke in 1985, it had thousands of taste test results saying people preferred the taste of the new product over the old. Yet sales crashed almost immediately and the company hurriedly reintroduced Classic Coke within weeks of abandoning it. It had failed to take into account that, even though people liked the taste of the new product better, it wasn't the taste of the Coke they had grown to love.

---

trends (or trends in customer complaints) based on the time of year. That can help you determine staffing or point you to marketing needs during off seasons.

Key Term **Aggregate Data** Data that has not been analyzed or put into any statistical format. It's also called *raw numbers*.

Statistical Significance A measure of how likely the data from a sampling is going to represent the data from the entire group. Usually the larger the sample, the more statistically significant the data.

Ethics and Legalities of Data Use

Remember that you can use the information you've obtained directly from a customer only for the purpose you've told him or her. You cannot sell it to other companies or use it for future research projects unless you have the customer's informed consent.

Manager's Checklist for Chapter 5

❑ Let your business and CRM strategies guide your need for data and information.

❑ Data will point to the information you need.

❑ Data helps you identify trends.

❑ Information helps you spot specific business issues.

❑ Tell employees what they need to know about how the data will be used.

❑ Provide database access only to those who truly need it.

❑ Maintain and respect customer privacy at all times.

❑ Look at ways to merge and cross-reference the data.

Tools for Capturing Customer Information

You know what data and information you want. You know
what you'll do with it once you get it. You know who'll have
access to it and how you'll maintain customer privacy. But how,
in the 21st century information economy, do you begin to get
that information? Do you have to spend a lot of money? Is
"canned" data worthless? How can you get just what you need
without being swamped by meaningless statistics? And what if
your customers won't cooperate?

Yes, customer data and information collection is enough to
make the savviest manager tear out his or her hair. There are so
many options—and so little time to make decisions that can
spell success or death for your business.

Where to Get the Data and Information

The most efficient way to narrow your options is to look at the
advantages of each source of data. Generally, as the data and
information become more tailored to your business and more
accurate, they also become harder and more expensive to
obtain. Here's a list of common sources of customer information:

Government reports. City, county, state, and federal governments all produce demographic reports based on geography. You can easily find out—usually for no money—such information as how your community has changed

> **Avoid Information Overload**
>
> "The biggest problem facing American business today is that most managers have too much information. It dazzles them, and they don't know what to do with it all."
> —Lee Iacocca

over the years and what the government experts feel trends in major industries will be. The disadvantage is that the data is generic and tells you very little about your specific customers and prospects.

Private reports. There are many companies that provide detailed information on populations based on ZIP code or telephone prefix. Unlike the government data, they will give more precise information on education level, age, income, average length of tenure in the neighborhood, type of employment, and other statistics that can help a local business pinpoint trends that could affect marketing efforts.

Trade associations. Many trade associations conduct yearly surveys to determine trends in their industry. These will detail how the industry is changing, who the key players are, and what's expected for the future. They're a perfect starting place, so don't ignore them, but remember that this information is available to all your competitors too.

Point of sale. Even the smallest company with little or no IT technology will keep some records based on sales transactions. A friend who holds several garage sales a year knows that the best days are Thursdays in her neighborhood; after a couple years, she quickly learned not to bother with the weekends.

But technology allows extremely sophisticated POS (point of sale) information—computerized cash registers can record the time of day, the exact products purchased, how the customer paid for the merchandise, and the size of transaction. These systems will generate reports that can help you predict staffing levels and provide inventory control tools. At the same time, these systems frequently allow you to input basic information at the time of sale such as a ZIP code, a telephone number, or the gender of the customer.

Similar systems are available for business-to-business sales. Some allow the salesperson to input data from a laptop computer the second a contract is signed. Others require clerical workers to input the information from invoices. Help desk software tracks transactions through "trouble tickets."

Whether you use sophisticated technology or the bare-bones "eyeball" method, this is the first stage in getting real information about your specific customers.

Employees. In Chapter 5 we talked about how to motivate front-line staff to obtain information and salespeople to share their information about the customers. These two groups—as well as other employees—are the next logical step in obtaining "passive" customer information. Employees become your eyes and ears as they communicate with customers.

> **Key Term**
>
> **Passive Information**
> Useful data that the customer doesn't know he or she is supplying. Some clothing retailers note how expensive their customers' jewelry is. Car salespeople will note what vehicle the customer's spouse drives. Comments such as "It took me forever to find this on the shelf" frequently are recorded as passive information.

For example, business-to-business salespeople frequently visit their customers' offices. They note how busy the production plants are at different times of the day, if the customer is adding production space, and if there's a sense of optimism in the air.

Retail employees can record how often customers ask to pay with a credit card the business doesn't take, how often customers ask for products the store doesn't carry, or how often customers become frustrated because they can't find something.

The value of this information is that it can be communicated directly to the people in your organization who most need it.

"Just Let Us Know ...."

A small computer components manufacturer wanted to discover what it could do about customer complaints that deliveries weren't arriving on time. Instead of chastising the delivery department, it brought in several delivery employees to meet with several salespeople. The salespeople were able to explain that certain products had to be delivered within 12 hours because they were key components to industrial systems that would idle the customers' factories if they weren't working. Salespeople were supposed to put a "rush" on these orders, but sometimes they forgot and sometimes the instructions were ignored. Other products could be delivered in two or three days with no concern.

The delivery department reacted by creating a two-tiered system. Instead of shipping all items first-order in, first-order out, they created a list of items that always went out immediately. If it meant some less important items had to wait until the next day, that was OK because the customers didn't care.

Have the salespeople sit down with the delivery people. Have the product engineers sit down with the customer service department. Suddenly your employees are sharing customer information they didn't even know they had.

Surveys. Surveys are a wonderful way to find out exactly what your customers are thinking about something. They range from very informal surveys of one or two questions to elaborate telephone surveys conducted by professional research firms. The larger the sample, the more you can extrapolate the results to the rest of your customers. However, even a small sample can point to areas that you need to examine further.

Simple, Crafty Survey

A major crafts retailer wanted to know if it was worthwhile to develop a Web site from which customers could directly purchase products. So, sales clerks asked each customer for one week if they ever bought anything over the Internet and, if so, would they buy fabric, yarn, or other craft supplies that way?

Yes, it was informal, but when more than half the customers said they'd probably buy some things that way, this retailer knew how it should proceed.

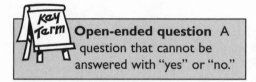

Open-ended question A question that cannot be answered with "yes" or "no."

Many surveys will have customers rank the importance of something or give a simple yes or no answer. Even if you've never conducted a survey, you're no doubt familiar with them from being a survey respondent at one time or another, especially during election season. As in the case of the crafts store, the data from closed-ended questions can confirm or point to logical next actions.

Open-ended questions, on the other hand, can provide even more valuable insight into what the customer really wants from his or her relationship with you. This is especially valuable if you're looking at a small group of people. For example, car dealerships frequently will survey in-depth the people who buy cars valued at more than $60,000 and those who have purchased more than three cars from the dealership in the last 10 years.

Focus groups. As with surveys, focus groups can run the gamut from an informal lunch with key customers to highly sophisticated, professionally run meetings with statistically selected customers. Focus groups are excellent for getting at complex problems or for general brainstorming—finding out in general what people think of a product or service. However, unless you conduct many such groups, your sample will be too small to really learn how the market is changing or what your typical customer feels.

CAUTION!

Ask the Right Questions

When using surveys, be wary of asking a question incorrectly or not asking it at all. Kristin Anderson worked with a hospital using a nationally normed customer satisfaction survey to find out what pleased patients and family members and what might make them prefer other hospitals. The widespread survey examined everything from staff helpfulness to the quality of the food. They forgot one question, though: Were you able to easily find your way through the hospital? Focus groups later revealed that "wayfinding" is an important factor when customers evaluate their overall hospital experience.

Give a Little to Get a Lot

Customers don't necessarily like to give you information about themselves. If you find they balk at your survey, offer an incentive, such as a coupon for 40% off their next purchase, an opportunity to win a trip, or a token of appreciation. In business-to-business settings, a personal incentive isn't always appropriate. Consider instead offering to make a donation to a charity.

How Far Do I Need to Go?

There's no rule about how to get your customer information. The important thing is that you get some information and start using it to help your employees become more aware of how important the information can be. Don't worry

Better to Ask for Permission than Forgiveness

If you're asking customer for their e-mail addresses, do not assume they are giving you permission to contact them that way. You must ask for that permission at the time you solicit the information.

too much at first about it being extremely accurate. Just start getting into the habit of collecting the information and using it.

When to Get What

Try narrowing your customer data and information collection efforts even further by collecting specific information at various points in the life cycle of a customer. Key contact points and the information you should collect at each include:

Customer Assistance

If you don't want to spend the time and money to conduct elaborate surveys with many open-ended questions, ask just a handful of your customers the open-ended questions. From their responses, you can design a check-off survey based on the most common answers.

1. Before you have customers. Use demographic and psychographic information to determine who your customers should be, how you will market your business, and what products and services are important to offer.

Start Small

Smart Managing   Choose three key customer segments and hold focus groups to find out what they like and don't like about your business. Those groups could be:
- Top spenders
- Long-time customers
- Recent defectors to your competitors

What Do Customers Really Want?

Long before Saturn Corporation introduced any cars to the marketplace, it held focus groups with people who'd recently bought cars. Among the questions asked was "What did you dislike most about the sales transaction?" When women overwhelmingly responded that they hated haggling over the price, the company knew it had a unique marketing niche and the "one-price, no-haggling" concept of car purchasing was born.

2. Initial contact with a customer or prospect. People don't have to buy something to be considered customers for information purposes. A simple written or in-person survey can help you find out the following:
- How they heard about your operation (good for marketing information)
- What their first impression is
- How much effort they exerted to contact you (how far they drove if you're a retailer; whether they used a magazine reply card, Internet search, or other source if you're in business-to-business sales)
- Where they currently get similar products and services
- What they would like to see you offer (in other words, what they like about your competitors)

3. Early in the relationship. After the first purchase, you can begin developing a database on the specific customer. Begin by recording information such as:
- When the purchases are made
- How they are paid for
- Any specific requests
- How large the purchases are
- What exactly was purchased

What's It Worth to You?

TRICKS OF THE TRADE

A good rule of thumb for how much to spend on a data and information collection effort is to look at the cost of the decisions that will come out of it and plan about 10% of that cost to procure the knowledge.

For example, if your sales have gone down $1 million during the last year, expect to spend about $100,000 to find out why that happened and what you can do to remedy it.

If you're looking to spend about $50,000 to develop a Web site so your business-to-business customers can order directly any time day or night, plan to spend about $5,000 up front to make sure they'll use it. If you want to know generally how you can improve your business by retaining customers, calculate how much customer defection cost you last year and budget 10% of that cost for your research efforts.

- Any complaints
- How the customer contacts you

4. Later in the relationship. While this varies widely from one business to another, virtually every businessperson knows his or her "good" customers. The retailer knows which faces he or she sees again and again. The industrial salesperson knows who buys the most and has the fewest complaints. Select these people for specific surveys or focus groups to discover:

- Industry trends
- Problems with your organization that could cause defections
- Trends in products, purchasing methods, delivery methods, or other components of the customer relationship

5. At a pause in the relationship. Many businesses have times when a customer naturally falls from their active list, especially when the business has an Hourglass Customer Service/ Sales Profile. Realtors, for example, don't expect to see the same faces every month. Bridal shops don't expect to see their customers again—for at least a couple years. However, that doesn't mean they stop being customers. These people are an important source of business referrals and

> **TRICKS OF THE TRADE**
>
> ### Add Advisors to Your Team
>
> Many businesspeople conduct ongoing focus groups with key customers under the guise of a "customer advisory council." When you treat them like advisors, customers often are motivated to give more information. They also have a reason to stay loyal to the company.

future business. After all, people buy bigger houses when they have children and brides may have friends or daughters who become brides. When natural pauses occur, use a survey or focus group to discover what the customer liked and disliked about the entire process of working with you. Use the data from these transactions as comparisons for upcoming months and years.

6. At the end of the relationship. If a customer stops doing business with you, he or she is a key source of information. Use a survey to find out:

- If there was a customer service problem
- If your products no longer met their needs
- Who they started doing business with instead of you
- If the reason was unrelated to your relationship (they moved to another state)

The Computer Is Your Friend (but Not Always Your Best Friend)

There is no question that computers have changed the world of customer relationship management. They not only provide the means to obtain much of the data, but also store the data and generate reports based on the data. There's nothing so wonderful as the number-generating potential of a large database with a savvy IT person at the helm.

Yet that doesn't mean it's right for you. As we've mentioned through this chapter and Chapter 5, the goal is not to see how much information you can get on your customers; it's to get information that is useful to you and your coworkers. That doesn't always necessitate a huge database. In fact, sometimes

---

Low-Tech Workaround

The customer service manager at a large mail order company became concerned when employees said they'd been getting a number of calls complaining about incorrect sales tax being added to their invoices. The sophisticated database only allowed the customer service worker to enter a code for "invoice dispute," not for the specifics of the dispute. As a result, this manager armed her employees with pads of paper and pencils. Every time they received a complaint about sales tax, they simply made a mark on the paper. At the end of a month, she tallied up the complaints and took the number to the accounting department. Her approach might not have been high-tech, but it got the job done.

---

it means just a sheet of paper and a pencil.

For that reason, keep these things in mind when planning your database, whether it's a subset of a large corporate database or the entire system for a company:

1. Small computers have big capabilities. Basic programs such as Word® or Excel® can tabulate data and present it in charts. A software designer can inexpensively create a database specifically for your company that will run on a typical PC and generate reports on key customer interactions as well as cross-reference basic customer facts such as customer ZIP code and average purchase.

2. Even the best system can't do it all. Many large corporations have elaborate customer information databases, but they can't always capture the information your individual department needs. Think outside the database box for the best way to get the information as quickly as possible.

3. You get what you ask for. Computers don't know what you want; they know only what you actually ask for. Computers are literal and do just what you tell them to do. As a result, it's important to have some basic training on your specific database system if you plan to ask for tailored reports. If you're having a system built for you, make sure you've included all the basic reports in your specs.

CAUTION!

Query Right

A query is a way of asking a computerized database for a report. Knowing how to query to get cross-referenced information or small subsets of data can take some practice and the tutelage of the software designer. If you don't do it right, you won't get the information you want.

Believe It or Not

You can prove anything with statistics. Want to prove that the world is flat? Just ask a mathematician and you'll have the proof. How about proving that bees can't actually fly? Ask an aeronautical engineer. Or perhaps you're out for evidence that your customers all love you? No problem. Just tell the database manager that's what you want and the proof will be on your desk in the morning.

Virtually all of us have grown up in a world jaded by numbers. There are books written about how to lie with statistics. (Whether we attribute it to Benjamin Disraeli, Mark Twain, Winston Churchill, or anybody else, we tend to accept as truth the statement, "There are lies, damn lies, and statistics.") We've seen politicians warp numbers until the facts are unrecognizable. We've probably even fudged a few numbers in our own lives and quickly learned that no one (such as the IRS?) was the wiser.

Add to this a healthy dose of life experience. For instance, after 30 years working in this industry, your marketing manager *knows* how to reach your customers. Anyone from the GI Generation (the group that came of age during the Great Depression and World War II) *knows* that price is the most important attribute for any product. Your much younger customer service people *know* that people get impatient if they have to wait more than a minute, that time is the most important attribute. And you *know* that none of that is a given.

Price and time may both be important. Or neither may matter much. If you really want to find out what matters to your customers, you have to be willing to let go of what you think you know and to ask your customers.

So, you've collected the real data and information, but others still cling to their personal views. As a manager, how can you convince the people making business decisions that the data is valid? In a world of number-weary professionals, that can be the biggest challenge of any CRM effort. These tactics will make that challenge a little easier:

1. Ask for input up front. If you'll be asking people to use this information, make sure they have a say in how it's collected. Have them review surveys, sit in on focus groups, or even work the POS to make sure they're comfortable with the procedure. Get their buy-in in the beginning so they can't complain about the data once it comes in.

2. Create the tools that ensure consistency. Don't just tell your salesclerks to ask for certain information. Provide an actual script for them. Develop forms that make it easy for them to jot down the answers. Train them on how to ask for the information.

3. Recognize that it is work. If you're asking your employees to ask questions or even supply information they have in their files, you're asking for extra effort. The information will be of better quality and more reliable if you let them know you're aware of the effort. For example, if you want telephone customer service people to add a question to each call, remember that their per-day call average likely will go down during the survey period.

Try gathering the information over a specified period of time, so the employees know when their extra effort will be finished. Also offer a little incentive, such as an hour of vacation or a prize for the person with the most surveys.

4. Use those open-ended questions. Verbatim comments can bring customers to life and make them more real for employees who don't have routine customer contact. When a salesperson hears a customer saying he or she doesn't care about price as much as quality and performance, the information sinks in much faster than reading a report that says 67% of customers rank quality as more important than price.

To provide powerful quotes, record focus groups or telephone surveys and have them edited for the strongest comments, then play them for employees or have the comments transcribed for bigger groups.

5. Tabulate the open-ended questions. A common response to many surveys containing open-ended questions is "But that's just one person." Professional survey firms will put responses into several categories and give you data based on those wordy comments.

6. Don't view it in black and white. Each customer has a different perception of an event or product based on his or her expectations—and those expectations can change by the second. For example, if you're in a hurry and stop at the local diner for lunch, a two-minute wait to get seated is definitely poor customer service. If you're waiting for a friend and have planned a leisurely lunch, those same two minutes can seem pretty speedy. The weather, the customer's personal life, and virtually everything happening in the world at the second you asked a question can have an impact on the answer. Remember that when looking at individual comments.

7. Ask why. If the data is contradictory with something you know to be true, ask yourself why that might be. It could be that you forgot a key question, such as the hospital that forgot to ask patients and visitors about the ease of finding their way around. It could be that you have an imperfect sample of customers—retailers who survey only between 10 a.m. and 4 p.m. likely won't get full-time white-collar workers in their samples. And never forget: it also could be that what you thought was true simply isn't.

> ## A Big Frenzy but No Trend
>
> In the three months leading up to January 1, 2000, sales of diesel generators skyrocketed in the northern United States. If managers at hardware and fleet and farm stores had looked at those numbers as a trend, they would have been more than tripling their orders the next fall. Lucky for most of them that they were well aware of the millennium hysteria that caused people to buy such products in case the electricity failed.

Manager's Checklist for Chapter 6

❑ Use different tools to get different data and information.

❑ The more time-consuming and expensive the tool, the better the resulting information.

❑ Collect different information at different stages in the customer relationship.

❑ Sometimes you have to throw out the computer.

❑ Use tactics that ensure employees will believe the data.

Service-Level Agreements

"'SLA' is just a new-age term for the age-old telecom contract," writes Julie Bort in her article, "SLA Savvy, Five Secrets for Making Sure You Get the Most from Your Service-Level Agreements" (*Network World*, September 27, 1999). And she's right. However, today service-level agreements cover much more than telecommunications. SLAs can also be found in IT (information technology), ASP (application service providers), and ISP (Internet service providers) agreements. And, whether you enter into a formal contract or use the concept in informal partnership discussions, understanding SLAs can help you ensure that everyone in your team is on board and contributing to your customer relationship management strategy.

Service-Level Agreements Defined

In the words of Joel Snyder of *Network World*, an SLA "is really just a description of the service you've bought and paid for...." While Joel is literally correct, an SLA implies—and spells out in detail—something more. According to the ASP Industry

Consortium's *Buyer's Guide to Service-Level Agreements*, an SLA should include:

> **Service-level agreement** Key Term
> A promise or guarantee of performance between a service provider and a customer. Traditionally, SLAs are used in business-to-business settings, for agreements with telecommunication, IT (information technology), ASP (application service providers) and ISP (Internet service providers) firms.

- the purpose of the SLA,
- Description of service,
- Duration of service,
- Installation timetable,
- Payment terms,
- Termination conditions, and
- Legal issues such as warranties, indemnities, and limitation of liability.

The SLA, then, is a contract between the service provider and the customer—typically a business or organization, rather than an individual consumer.

Three Keys to Effective SLAs

Whether you're the service provider or the customer, a well thought out and clearly executed SLA can strengthen your relationship by setting reasonable expectations, clear measures of performance, and rewards when performance is excellent or remuneration if it falls short.

To see this more clearly, let's consider a typical consumer agreement for telephone service compared with a SLA between a telecom provider and a call center. Our examples look from the customer's point of view, but feel free to imagine yourself on either side of these agreements. Consider the role the agreement does or does not play in keeping the customer loyal.

Put on your consumer hat for a moment. As a residential customer, you have a service agreement with your local telecom provider. You agree to pay a certain amount per month and the provider agrees to give you a dial tone. You may also contract with this same provider for additional services, such as caller ID, last call return, phone or line repair, and the like. You decide to add a second line for your new home office. You call and to make an appointment for line installation. "Our technician will be there between 8 and noon."

You don't want to take the entire morning off work. Isn't a more definite appointment available?

"No. We'll call you when the technician is on the way. That's the best we can do."

So you take the morning off work, wait for the tech ... and wait ... and wait. At 11:50, you call the dispatcher for a status check ... again.

"Oh, the other job ran long. The tech won't be able to make it. We'll have to reschedule. How about 8 a.m. to noon, a week from today?"

You may get angry, but short of switching service providers, there's not much you can do.

Now, put on your business hat. Your organization also contracts for telephone services. Let's imagine, for example, that you have a customer contact center where 105 service representatives handle incoming customer calls 24 hours a day, 7 days a week. It's imperative for your business that customers have 24/7 access, so you need a very high level of performance from your telecom provider. So, you establish a service-level agreement.

In it, you detail *accountability*. Is your provider just bringing a dial tone to your internal telecommunication system? Or is your provider responsible for ensuring that your internal telecommunication system is functioning correctly? What about third-party software or hardware? Will your provider take responsibility for telephone lines installed by another vendor? And what will the provider be responsible for if fire, flood, or an act of God interrupts your service?

Next, you detail *performance levels*. What amount of time, if any, is it acceptable for your phone connections to be "down"? How quickly will new lines be installed when you choose to expand your service? Every key aspect of performance is cov-

Accountability Responsibility. This part of the SLA defines what each party to the agreement—the service provider and the customer—is responsible for.

Performance levels Expectations for how the requirements of the agreement will be fulfilled.

Remuneration Compensation when performance fails to meet the agreed-upon level.

ered, in a quantifiable way, so you and the service provider know when the performance level is met and when performance is unsatisfactory.

Finally, you detail in your SLA *remuneration*. Remuneration is what the service provider promises to give you if it fails to meet performance levels. Usually, it's a percentage of the fee for service. This part of the SLA can also include rewards if the provider gives an exceptional level of service performance.

You want to bring in three new phone lines. You call and make an appointment. In accordance with your SLA, installing new lines of this type may take as long as 48 hours. Because the sooner the lines are in, the more the provider makes, the company has an incentive to do a speedy job—and it does, getting your new lines up and running less than 24 hours after your call.

As the customer, it's easy to see how the SLA benefits you. Thinking of the consumer example, you may even wish you had an SLA to hold over the head of your local telecom service provider. However, from the service provider's point of view, the SLA is more than a big stick wielded by customers to get performance.

Remember our definition of customer relationship management: a comprehensive approach for creating, maintaining, and expanding customer relationships. The crafting of the SLA provided an opportunity to create a customer relationship with reasonable and achievable expectations. It was a time for engaging the customer in the creation of a service plan that works for both the provider and the receiver. Clear expectations for both the everyday events of the service relationship, such as expanding service, and fallbacks and compensation for those times when, despite best efforts, things didn't work as we'd hoped, also keep the customer relationship on an even keel.

Creating an SLA

As a manager interested in promoting CRM, you may be on the provider or the receiver side of the SLA. Either way, the process for creating your service-level agreement remains the same, especially when the services you're contracting are tools to support your CRM strategy.

There are six steps to the SLA process map.

Step 1 in the process is to review your CRM strategy. Because SLAs are traditionally focused on *who* does *what* and *when*, it's critical to begin with *why* any of us are doing any of it. The key focus should always be to create and retain customers.

With a clear understanding of what you want to accomplish, you can move to **Step 2**: meet with the other party to define requirements and expectations. It's important to be extremely clear in your definitions because you and the other party—

⚠ CAUTION!   Don't Agree to Disservice Your Customers

Carol Kerr recently purchased a new computer. The retailer explained that she could order her PC direct from the manufacturer for $200 less than the cost of the display model. After receiving assurances that the computer would be ready by a specific date, Carol placed her order. When Carol called to check on the status of her computer a day before the promised delivery, she learned that the manufacturer was behind and hadn't even started to build her unit—and that it wouldn't be ready for at least two more weeks. Disappointed, but needing her new PC, Carol offered to pay the extra $200 and take the floor model. "Oh, we can't do that. You can't cancel an order once it's been placed." After several conversations, a few heated words, and two calls between the manager and the manufacturer, Carol was able to give the store $200 more and take home the floor model. This is a clear case where the SLA between the reseller and the manufacturer must have made sense to someone—but in the end it didn't build customer relationships for either of them.

Motorola Uses Analogies

Smart Managing

Use analogies and examples to enhance understanding for your requirements and expectations. For example, a project group at Motorola needed to create a new agreement with a key customer for prioritizing crises. "Every week, or more often even, they would call with a new crisis—often caused by something that happened on their end. And they expected us to drop everything and move mountains. And we did, but we did it so often we were actually creating more crises on our side. It was a vicious circle. Everything was becoming a crisis."

The team leader set up a meeting with his customer. We coached him to use the language with the customer that he'd used with us. In the meeting, he explained to his counterpart, "We can move mountains, just not every mountain, every day." The image added both humor and clarity to the discussion. And the customer agreed to prioritize and expect "only two mountains moved by miracle each month."

whether a service provider or a customer—may have different worldviews.

Don't leave any expectation or requirement unstated. Walk together through the service process. What will it look like, feel like, sound like when everything is going well? What types of issues or service interruptions might you anticipate and how should those be handled? See Chapter 9, Managing Relationships Through Conflict, for more on handling possible service problems.

Questions to Ask

MISTAKE PROOFING

To help you anticipate problems, use this checklist. For each item, ask yourself, "What performance problems might occur around this issue?" If a performance problem is *likely* or if it puts your customer relationships at *extreme risk*, then it should be part of your requirements and expectations discussion.
• Personnel
• Facilities
• Power
• Internet/telecommunications connections
• Merger/acquisition
• Disaster

When you think you've defined the key performance requirements and expectations, check again with your CRM strategy. Will this performance truly help you achieve your CRM goals?

When both sides have agreed upon the key performance requirements and expectations, you're ready for **Step 3**: define performance measures. How will you determine if the agreed-upon performance level is being met? Measures should be timely and accurate, without placing any undue burden on anyone.

If your SLA concerns an application, you may measure performance with an application monitoring tools. This software solution can detect and record problems, identify slowdowns, and run in-depth reports on transactions and response time. If human performance is at issue, you may need both quantitative and qualitative measures. Again, compare your performance measures with your CRM strategy. Are your measures getting at the performance elements that most promote your CRM approach?

⚠ CAUTION!

Hanging Up

Operators at a service repair call center were measured on length of call. Ostensibly, the purpose of this measure was to create call efficiency, to discourage calls that were unnecessarily lengthy and chatty. In reality, the operators knew that at three minutes, the red light on their phones would begin to blink. Some, while in mid-word, would choose that moment to hang up on the customer. Their reasoning: "The customer would never believe I hung up on purpose while I was speaking and management would never believe that I needed more than three minutes to get all the information from the customer. But I did and I do. Hanging up just seems like the best option."

Do your performance measures inadvertently encourage the wrong performance?

Step 4, define rewards and penalties, goes hand in hand with Step 3. The performance measure means little until it's used to give rewards or to make corrections. Traditional SLAs focus on remuneration, on what the service provider will give back if performance falls short. Little, if any, attention is given to rewards for great performance.

"The reward is, they get to keep the contract," one manager told us. "Why should I give them extra if they do what they said they would do?"

Good point, but what about those times when the service provider goes above and beyond? You may want to be more creative in defining rewards. For example, you could ask for a letter of acknowledgment and praise that you can share with the service team ... or even use in marketing. The key is taking this opportunity to define ways to draw customer attention to superior performance.

Before leaving Step 4, compare your remuneration and reward agreements with your CRM strategy. Are you penalizing any behavior that may actually promote your CRM strategy? Are you rewarding any behavior that doesn't serve your CRM strategy?

Now you're ready for implementation, **Step 5**, monitor performance. Here's where the rubber meets the road. You've defined expectations and requirements, set up measures, and decided what you're going to do—to reward or to correct—based on the results. Put the process into motion and watch it go.

> **Don't Buy the Problem**
>
> **CAUTION!**
>
> "Buying the problem."
> That's the automotive industry's phrase for those times when they just give the customer money to go away, rather than fixing their automobile. In the automotive world, this strategy makes sense. There are some lemon cars that just can't be fixed to the customer's satisfaction. However, in an SLA, beware of the temptation to just "pay the price" and settle for performance that doesn't meet the mark. Yes, you will be in compliance with your agreement, but you won't be winning the long-term loyalty of your customer.

Keep your CRM strategy in mind as you review your monitoring efforts. Are you the monitoring police or the performance partner? We believe that your monitoring process can and should actually model the types of relationship you wish to promote with your customers.

The final step, **Step 6**, is to review the SLA regularly, at

Monitoring Adults

At a managed health care provider based in Minneapolis, member services representatives are regularly monitored for quality of calls. A computer system randomly samples their calls for a supervisor to review and grade. However, representatives who've proven themselves by earning consistently high ratings can monitor their own calls; the supervisor makes just a few spot checks each year. This process ensures quality and models an attitude that "we treat people as valued, capable adults." What does your monitoring process model?

least annually. The first year, we recommend that you review the agreement even more often, so you can make any needed adjustments in expectations and requirements. Sometimes it's only after an SLA is in place that you realize that a measure is sending performance in the wrong direction or that your monitoring process is too cumbersome to provide timely information.

Equally important in this step is realizing that your CRM strategy may change over time, so you'll need to adjust your SLA to stay current with it. The following box summarizes the steps we've just discussed.

Creating an SLA Process Map

Step 1: Review your customer relationship management strategy.

Step 2a: Meet to define requirements and expectations.

Step 2b: Compare to your CRM Strategy. Do the requirements you set truly help you achieve your CRM goals?

Step 3a: Define performance measures.

Step 3b: Compare your performance measures with your CRM strategy. Do your measures get at the performance elements that most promote your CRM approach?

Step 4a: Define rewards and penalties.

Step 4b: Compare your remuneration agreement with your CRM strategy. Are you penalizing any behavior that may promote your CRM strategy? Are you rewarding any behavior that doesn't serve your CRM strategy?

Step 5a: Monitor performance.

Step 5b: Review your monitoring efforts while considering your CRM strategy. Are you modeling the type of relationship you wish to promote?

Step 6a: Review the SLA annually.

Step 6b: Note any changes to your CRM strategy. How must the SLA change to stay current with your CRM strategy?

Using SLAs to Support Internal Customer Relationships

Used with your internal customer relationships, SLAs can help you achieve two of the CRM success factors listed in Chapter 1:

1. Builds strong internal partnerships around the CRM strategy.
2. Employees at all levels and all areas accurately collect information for the CRM system.

As we stated in Chapter 1, CRM is everyone's responsibility. "CRM does not belong just to sales and marketing. It is not the sole responsibility of the customer service group. Nor is it the brainchild of the information technology team. ... CRM must be a way of doing business that touches all areas." Internal SLAs can help other areas know exactly how they support CRM.

For example, imagine that you're the manager of the customer service group. Your relationship to your organization's CRM strategy seems pretty clear. Your group is in contact with customers every day, using CRM tools to track each transaction, spot new trends as customer expectations change, and identify opportunities to expand the service relationship.

In addition to your contact with external customers, your group has internal service relationships with many other areas, including the warehouse. After reading this chapter, you decide to create an SLA with this group. As internal partners, you recognize that the agreement will involve performance-level expectations on both sides. You'll bring your concerns and invite your counterparts to bring theirs. You're there to discuss what you expect and what you need, so that at the end of the day external customers are well served. CRM, serving customers so well that they want to continue to do business with you and to find new ways to do business with you, is the touchstone for a good agreement.

For example, one of Kristin Anderson's clients recently installed a new CRM software tool to track customer problems. Customer service representatives were instructed to open a ticket for each customer incident. Some incidents were complex and needed to be escalated to the engineering group for resolution. The engineers were good about acting to resolve the issue, but lousy about recording their actions and closing out the trouble ticket; it just seemed like unnecessary extra work to them.

The manager of the customer service group met with the engineering team. Without using the term "service-level agreement," he took them through the process during the meeting. Once they understood *why* the information on the trouble ticket was important and how it was used, they were much more willing to complete the *online* forms. In return, they asked that some of the forms be simplified and that the groups agree on some common shorthand ways of entering information. Recent monitoring shows that the engineers are following through on their performance commitments. The internal partnership between engineering and customer service is stronger than ever.

Your internal service-level agreement may not have the

Get Out of Jail Free

A conference attendee told us about his department manager's creative effort to develop better working relationships with other internal areas. The original corporate culture placed a lot of energy on blaming and berating other departments for problems—which did nothing to get issues resolved for customers. One day, the manager brought in the "Get out of Jail Free" cards from his family's Monopoly® game. The next time someone began yelling about a mistake and blaming his department, he pulled out a card, signed it, and handed it over. "I'm sorry there is a problem and I want to get it fixed, ASAP. And to make it up to you, here's this card. The next time your area makes a mistake, pull this out and we won't yell or gripe or complain. We'll just get to business finding a solution."

Do your internal service agreements allow you to "get of out jail" and get to business on behalf of your customers?

financial rewards or remunerations. However, you can be creative. Maybe you'll decide to reward superior performance on either side by hosting a pizza party in appreciation.

Making SLAs Work

Ideally, service-level agreements are a way to ensure that your performance enhances customer relationships. But SLAs aren't a substitute for the ongoing, day-to-day work of uncovering what your customers expect and need, and searching for new ways to provide it to them.

Service-level agreements don't work when:

- Compliance to the "letter of the law" in the agreement means more than serving the customer.
- Customer needs and expectations change, but the SLA doesn't.
- Penalties are ignored or seen as a "cost of doing business."
- Superior performance isn't recognized and acknowledged in a meaningful way.

Make sure that your formal and informal SLAs don't fall into one of these performance traps.

The SLA model—defining accountability, performance levels, and reward and remuneration—is a powerful tool for your customer relationship management efforts. We encourage you to take the SLA model and use it with your business-to-business customers, your consumer customers, and your internal customers.

Manager's Checklist for Chapter 7

❏ A service-level agreement is a promise or guarantee of performance between a service provider and a customer.

❏ SLAs can help you ensure that everyone in your team is on board and contributing to your customer relationship management strategy.

❏ An effective SLA will spell out accountability, performance levels, and remuneration.

❏ Creating an SLA is a six-step process: (1) review your customer relationship management strategy, (2) meet to define requirements and expectations, (3) define performance measures, (4) define rewards and penalties, (5) monitor performance, (6) review. At each step of the way, use your CRM strategy as a touchstone to ensure that your efforts will serve to maintain and grow customer relationships.

❏ SLAs with internal customers can help you create strong internal partnerships around the CRM strategy and can encourage employees at all levels and all areas to collect accurate information for the CRM system.

E-Commerce: Customer Relationships on the Internet

Just a few years ago, Kristin Anderson attended a Chapter Leadership session at the National Speakers Association conference. As Director of Communications for the Minnesota Chapter, Kristin was looking for ways to get more information to chapter members—her NSA-MN "customers"—while spending less of their money. During a round-table discussion, Kristin learned that several chapters had done away with expensive printed newsletters in favor of e-zines or Web-based publications.

"But what about members who don't have e-mail?" she asked.

There was a moment of pause, then the discussion leader replied, "Our chapter doesn't have any members who don't have e-mail." Kristin just stared.

He went on to explain, "We used to have members who didn't have e-mail. Some of them just didn't think they needed it—they had ample business and their customers weren't complaining. Others didn't want to make the financial investment. And some were just plain afraid of the Internet. But a couple of years ago we made a decision to walk the talk of our mission, to 'advance the art and value of experts who speak professionally.' We challenged all our members to move into the electronic age and offered assistance and advice to those who were unsure. Today, not every chapter member has—or needs—a Web page marketing their services, but every member can and does communicate with clients, and colleagues via e-mail."

A leader from another chapter concurred: "Electronic communication is a must. You won't be taken seriously in this business or any business without it." The message was clear: if you want to be a business professional, you need to be on the information superhighway, the Internet.

A few years ago, we were inclined to argue that not every business needs to take this road. Today, we are hard-pressed to find examples of thriving businesses that don't drive on the information superhighway in one way or another. In fact, we are prepared to argue that e-commerce is a nonnegotiable if you want to maximize your CRM success—no matter what your business.

You have to understand enough about the Internet to understand how e-commerce changes and will continue to change your customers' expectations—and how it is changing their relationships with other service providers. As you will read in Chapter 10, Fighting Complacency, you are in competition with every other customer service provider your customer experiences.

Who's Using the Internet? Virtually Everyone

Consider this. Any one of us can download the federal tax forms we need from the IRS Web site. Is everybody doing so? No. Many taxpayers don't have Internet access or they find the prospect of searching the Web site to be intimidating. So, they continue to rely on the forms they get in the mail or from local libraries and post offices. However, a human resources manager recently shared with us, "I got my forms from someone who used the IRS Web site."

So, even those people who are just passengers are using the superhighway. And many of them are easing into taking the wheel. You want to be out there and ready for them.

CRM on the Internet

E-commerce really isn't a new game. It's an extension of the game we've been playing since the dawn of commerce—the game of creating, maintaining, and expanding customer relationships. Kristin Anderson's grandfa-

> **Customers on the 'Net**
>
> According to Nielsen/Net Ratings, 167.5 million people in the United States have home Internet access. That's nearly 60% of all Americans—and the number is rapidly growing across all demographic groups. Additionally, nearly half of all Americans buy on line. Can you really afford not to be on the 'Net?

Smart Managing

ther, whom we wrote about in the Preface, never knew about e-commerce. However, if Carl T. Anderson were running a grain elevator today, he would find the Internet to be a powerful tool for communicating with co-op members, watching the market for pricing trends, scheduling shipments, and completing sales.

To play the game of business in this century, it's important to know what e-commerce can do for you and how it's changing customer expectations. Working with the touchstone of your CRM strategy, you'll be able to use new rules and the new tools offered by e-commerce to satisfy your customers.

The Internet can enable your customer relationship management strategy in three ways.

Level 1: Getting information out to customers. The Internet can provide an avenue for getting information about your business and your products and services to your current and potential customers. At its most basic level, this means letting them know you are there and how to reach you in the "real world." It can be as simple as a Web-based brochure that describes your products and services and tells customers where you are located and how to reach you by phone.

Level 2: Getting information back from customers. The next level of sophistication means you not only provide information to your customers, but also learn more about them and from them. The Internet allows you to collect all sorts of useful—and sometimes not so useful—data about your customers.

Sometimes this means customers respond to questions and provide you useful information. In other cases you may be able to collect information that's very useful to your business without interfering at all with the customer experience.

Level 3: E-commerce sales. At its highest level, you can use the Internet to deliver products and services to your customers. You can have mutually rewarding relationships with customers you never see, meet, or speak with! Your entire relationship can successfully exist in cyberspace. With the technology available today, you can sell your products over the Internet, respond to customer questions, offer additional products and services based on previous purchases, and evaluate customers' satisfaction with your offerings—all without ever dealing with them in person. Leveraging the Internet can free up resources to deliver higher levels of value to customers in new ways.

Level 1: Getting Information out to Customers

With half of American households wired to the Internet, and the numbers growing throughout the United States and the world, you should expect your customers to search the Web for information about you and your products and services. From a CRM standpoint, it's helpful to think about this level of Internet activity in two ways, *passive* and *active*.

Whether you intend it or not, whether you create it or it comes from another source, we're willing to bet dollars to donuts that you have a presence on the Internet. A search of the Internet may reveal your passive presence in any number of ways. Here are just a few:

- Electronic Yellow Pages, such as www.SuperPages.com
- Conversations in an online chat or on an industry- or association-based bulletin board
- References in articles

While you don't directly control these sources of information—what we consider your *passive* Internet presence—it pays to be aware of what your customers will find when they look around the superhighway for you. If you find that negative information is out there, what Melinda Goddard of Roche Diagnostics calls "word of mouse," then you can plan a strategy to rebut it direct-ly or to arm your customer contact employees to address it if customers bring it up.

Keep Up to Date

Search for your company's contact information through several online yellow or business page sites. Most of these sites want to hear from you if your information is missing or inaccurate. Be proactive in keeping it up to date.

Smart Managing

You can also have an active Internet presence at Level 1 by putting up a simple, information-based Web page or by placing articles on sites your customers and potential customers are likely to visit. The key is to put your information where customers and potential customers will find it and use it to do business with you. After all, the core of CRM is creating, maintain-ing, and expanding cus-tomer relationships. You can't do that if they can't find you.

Check Your Signposts

When customers search for your company through the elec-tronic Yellow Pages or in a general Internet search, how quickly does your information appear? Make it a point to conduct a monthly Internet search for your company contact information.

Mistake Proofing

Level 2: Getting Information Back from Customers

The next level is to use the Internet to get information back from your customers. There are three general ways to do this.

First, you can simply have an e-mail address and make it available to your customers. For exam-ple, at the www.briefcase-books.com site, you can click on info@cwlpub.com to ask a general question

Having a Presence

You don't have to have your own Web page to have an Internet presence. For example, many small bed and breakfast operators have Internet listings with their area B&B association or with their local chamber of commerce.

Tricks of the Trade

> ### Take Our Challenge
> **TRICKS OF THE TRADE** Log onto an Internet search engine. Do a search using your company or product name. Browse through the results and then ask yourself these questions:
> - How easy is it for a customer to find and contact you via the Internet?
> - Are there any other companies or Web sites with similar names that might confuse your customers?
> - How could you make it easier for customers to find you through an Internet search?
>
> A quick search of "briefcase books" on www.google.com brought up the home page for this book series—www.briefcasebooks.com—as the first entry. However, it also brought up a site for a software company that has a page recommending fiction books, a possible source of confusion for readers and potential readers of this series.

or send a suggestion to John Woods and the team at CWL who put the series together in partnership with McGraw-Hill. Or you may click on the *Motivating Employees* book and send a question or comment directly to co-author Anne Bruce.

> ### Ask the Experts
> Kristin Anderson adds to her active Internet presence by participating in the "Ask the Experts" network through www.TrainingSuperSite.com. Every time she chooses to answer a question and it's posted on the site, Kristin increases her visibility to clients and potential clients. Where could you or a member of your team increase your Internet presence? And if you serve internal customers, where could you increase your presence on your organization's intranet?

Second, you can also collect information from your customers by asking them to register at your site. The registration process allows you to collect some general information up front. And, when customers log in on subsequent visits, Web-based software can track the way they use the site so you can learn about what information they seek out first and most often, what areas of your site they don't bother to visit, and how frequently they stop off at your Superhighway exit. If your customers might balk at signing in just to cruise your site, you can use CRM software tools to track them based on their purchases.

A third way to collect data from your customers is by putting surveys or a question of the day on your site. It also serves to actively engage them in your site. And offering to e-mail them the results or to post the results on your Web page gives you another opportunity to communicate with this key group.

> ### Use Your Databases
> Smart Managing
>
> Make sure that customer purchase tracking tools integrate with other customer databases. For example, in collecting past-due payments from a customer, it makes business sense to offer more leeway to a long-term customer who always pays, albeit off schedule.

Level 3: E-Commerce Sales

As organizations yearn to move beyond the traditional world of bricks and mortar, the call goes out: "Let's get on the Internet and sell stuff." We encourage you to walk before you run—or

> ### Check the E-Mail
> CAUTION!
>
> If you make an e-mail address available to your customers, make sure someone checks it regularly—several times a day is best. Customers expect quick replies to e-mail, even if that reply is simply "We got your message and will have an answer for you within 48 hours."

drive—on the e-commerce highway. Even if you launch all three levels at the same time, consider them in a linear fashion. It's important to know what information is already out there about you—or about your industry or service segment. And before you start charging credit cards and shipping products, it's vital that you have systems and processes in place to receive and answer customer questions and concerns.

There are two parts to a level-3 Internet presence.

One part is the actual sales of products and services. This is what comes to mind when we hear the term "e-commerce." Large-scale retailers use sophisticated applications to manage online sales. This requires a large investment and requires high-volume sales to make it pay off. If you aren't ready to be in e-commerce in such a dedicated way, you can still offer your products and service by linking to another e-commerce source. For example, many authors will link their personal sites to their book publisher's site or to a large book retailer, such as Amazon or 800-CEO-READ (formerly Schwartz Business Books).

The 'Net as Research

Smart Managing   Research suggests that up to 75% of online shoppers don't complete their purchase on the Internet. Instead they use e-commerce sites to find and research products before completing their purchase either by phone or with a visit to a store location.

The other part of your level-3 presence is providing real-time customer service support.

David Sims, writing in crmguru.com's *Customer Relationship Management Primer*, notes, "Every person who uses online help instead of calling you saves you money." He quotes a Web-based customer service application vendor who explains, "The whole point of online customer service—e-service—is to have people taking up your website's time instead of taking up your customer service reps' time."

Customer Service and E-Commerce

Smart Managing   Forrester Research found that 37% of all online buyers have requested customer service online. 90% of online shoppers consider good customer service to be critical when choosing a Web merchant. How good is your online customer service?

You can provide online customer service through the following means:

- *Search engines*—A site-based search engine helps your customer find answers to his or her questions, locate information, and connect quickly to the right department.
- *Frequently Asked Questions (FAQs)*—A place on your Web site where you list and respond to the most common concerns expressed by customers.
- *Live help*—Your customers can actually speak to a customer service representative while they're online visiting your site through Voice over Internet Protocol (VOIP) applications.

- *Online order tracking*—With customized applications, you can allow customers to track the progress of their order, just as Federal Express allows customers to check package status over the Internet.

Nazan Fathy, writing for www.suite101.com, "E-commerce: All About Customer Relationship Management" (April 1, 1999), said, "The epitome of online service is to respond to customers in a consistent and high-quality manner through their channel of choice, whether that is the e-mail, the phone or online chat."

> **Voice over Internet Protocol (VOIP)** A feature that allows visitors to a Web site to click a "call agent" button. If your customer has a multimedia PC, the service representative can have a conversation with the customer right over the Internet. Or, the customer may send a message for the service rep to call back on a separate line.
>
> *Key Term*

Choosing the Right Vehicle

Having a presence on the electronic superhighway doesn't require that you purchase a brand-new Lexus, but you should not assume that the cheapest model with no options will do the job. Choosing the right e-commerce vehicle for you and your customers is a three-step process.

Step one is to go back to your customer relationship management strategy. Refresh your memory. Ask yourself three questions:

1. What am I trying to accomplish with CRM?
2. What kind of experience(s) do I want my customers to have?
3. What information do I need to get to or from my customers to enable delivery of an exceptional customer experience?

We suggest that you keep a written copy of your CRM strategy close at hand as you work through the next two steps of the process. Make sure every decision you make along the way is aligned with your overall CRM strategy.

Step two is to plan out where you want to go. Think about the Customer Service/Sales Profile discussed in Chapter 2 and Chapter 3. Where do you want to take your customers during their online visit? Amazon.com uses its online presence to foster customer relationships at all three levels. Any individual can search the Amazon database and purchase a book or other product. That's the stand-alone transaction piece. Amazon also encourages your next purchase, the "repeat customer" piece, with its "customers who bought this product also bought these products" feature. When we visit Amazon.com, we are automatically recognized and greeted with "Hello. We have recommendations for you." Amazon.com also nurtures the "customer advocacy" piece by asking customers to review the books and products they find on its electronic pages. This invitation encourages customers to visit the site *after* they make and receive their purchase, just to put in their two cents about their satisfaction or dissatisfaction with what they received.

Taking its customers on this highly sophisticated road through the its Pyramid Profile requires that Amazon.com invest large amounts of financial and human capital in its e-commerce connections. Amazon's applications represent the monster SUV of e-commerce. And it works, and works well, for that company.

You, however, may want to begin with a more modest investment as you choose your e-commerce vehicle. Consider how your company and your department currently connect with customers. Think about your external customers—those who pay money for your products and services—and your internal customers—other departments or individuals who depend on you and your group.

Make a list. Put a star by the connections that already use the Internet. Here's our list to get you started:

- Yellow pages/phone directory: More and more customers search for company contact information via the Internet. Are you listed? Is the listing accurate and up to date?
- E-mail: Is your e-mail address easily available to your customers? Many organizations now use e-mail in the

same way that 800 numbers have been used for decades.

- Web site: Is your site passive, more of an electronic brochure for your products and services? Or does it allow customers to search for information and FAQs? Can customers buy directly via your Web site? Does your site help you learn more about what your customers are looking for?
- Live interaction via the Web site: Can customers connect with you while at your Web site by using document sharing or a VoIP?

Now, consider additional ways your customers may *want* to connect with you via the Internet.

Step three is to choose the e-commerce vehicle or fleet that best matches where you are and where you want to go. List all your options. Do your research. And consider the cost. Don't buy an application that you aren't financially prepared to staff and support. It's better to just have an e-mail address and a passive Web page than to invite customers to engage with you and make purchases at a site that doesn't run smoothly ... or at all. Remember that you can implement the e-commerce sales portion of your CRM strategy in stages. You don't have to do everything all at once.

> ### Nordstrom.com
>
> "We wanted something very interactive for our customers," said Paul Onnen, CTO of Nordstrom.com. "A lot of people have one phone line and they can't be on the Internet and call the customer service center at the same time. They don't want to wait for the turnaround of an e-mail; they want something simultaneous." VOIP was the answer according to an article in *InfoNews* by Bob Trott and Jessica Davis (December 11, 2000).

Three Rules for Success on the Road to E-Commerce

Now you're ready to rev up your e-commerce vehicle(s), whether e-mail, your Web site, or a sophisticated real-time interaction. Here's where many of us get distracted from our view of the forest by all those really cool trees out there! Throughout your e-commerce implementation, keep your focus by remembering three rules for success:

- E-commerce doesn't need to cost big bucks.
- Keep it current. Customers expect Internet data to be more current and up to date than any of your print materials.
- Strive to keep it personal.

CAUTION!

Don't Get Hung Up on Technology

E-commerce CRM applications grow out of the same strategy seed as all other CRM applications. Beware of technology for technology's sake. Know what channels your customers prefer and at what level of sophistication they use those channels. While the number of homes and businesses linked to us by the information superhighway rises, not everyone is driving a fast car. Just as we see old clunkers on the roadways, there are clunker computers/software out there. What speed are your core customers driving at? Can they load and use your e-application easily at that speed? Too many spinning graphics and the page won't load. And remember: you can't ask someone to look at your Web site as they talk to you on the phone if their Internet connection is using their phone line, and their computer can't handle VOIP.

E-Commerce Need Not Be Expensive

A simple page— an electronic brochure—that says you're out there in "space" and directs them to your "place" is better than no presence. Carol found a lovely bed and breakfast in Marion, S.C. while searching the Web for a hotel near Darlington for a planned visit to the spring NASCAR race. She made reservations over the phone and sent the deposit by "snail mail" because the B&B didn't accept credit cards, but it turned out to be the perfect place—30 minutes from the racetrack, homey, with opportunities to meet and visit with other race fans that she wouldn't have had at one of the big chain motels.

Keep It up to Date

This is not about being on the cutting edge of technology. This is about updating electronic information the same as you update information elsewhere. It takes more attention, though, because it's "out there"

New Customers
Minnesota Orchestral Association launched online ticket purchases just a few years ago. They found that this tapped a whole new group of patrons, individuals who regularly searched the Web for entertainment events and who now considered and attended concerts.

somewhere. It's not like your bricks-and-mortar presence: you walk though your facility, you handle papers, you see signage and realize it is wrong and needs to be changed and updated. But, just as we may forget to listen to our own voice mail message to test it, we forget to cruise and test our e-commerce connections. For example, a local restaurant still hadn't changed its Web information to the new area code, even two months after the old area code stopped working. The Web page invited guests to call the restaurant for reservations, but any potential customer who tried would get a "that number is no longer in service" message.

Make It Personal

Think about how each aspect of your Web site will either enhance or detract from the customer experience. Another way of thinking about it is to ask this question: Will what you're asking your customer to do make their lives better or easier in some way?

For example, Amazon.com allows Carol to add items to a "Wish List." That way when her parents or favorite aunt are looking for a gift idea, they can log onto the site and always find a list of things she would love to receive. They enter their credit card information and their gift is shipped directly to her doorstep. It's the equivalent of the bridal registry, even when you're not getting married! From the customer's standpoint, it's easy: Carol can add things as she is browsing—and her parents don't have to worry about going to the store, finding something they're not sure she will like, and then shipping it 1500 miles from North Dakota to Texas.

> **CAUTION!**
>
> ### Finding Service
>
> Bob Trott and Jessica Davis wrote about "Elusive Customer Service" in *InfoWorld* (December 11, 2000). One comment, by an industry analyst, is very striking: "More than 50% of Web sites don't have anything on their main page that tells customers where to go for service. That's abysmal. That's like walking into a brick-and-mortar store and not seeing any salespeople on the floor." How easy is it for your customers to locate service assistance on your Web site?

And what does Amazon.com get out of this? They now have information about items Carol is likely to purchase in the future, topics she's interested in, and products other customers like Carol may be interested in.

What Does the Future Hold?

"Customer contact means customer contact," she insisted. "The Internet can't replace that, can't substitute for that. Besides, only wealthy people can afford to have it." In 1988, we heard a lot of customer service managers talking that way. Today, bricks-and-mortar stores are converting to bricks-and-clicks entities at an amazing pace. Just look at the number of department stores that offer online shopping inside the store. They don't have it in stock? You'd rather have it delivered than schlep it home? You're buying a gift that you would like to send directly to the lucky recipient? Then just step up to the kiosk, activate the mouse, and begin shopping.

In fact, hold onto your mouse pad—there's a new evolution coming. We're going mobile. E-commerce is changing from bricks-and-clicks to place-and-space. No, physical store locations, factories, and distribution centers aren't going away. But not every business venture will need them. Yet almost all companies and organizations will need to create and manage electronic contacts with customers that work well on a cell phone or a handheld device.

In a recent Start the Week Inspiration Pack, eCustomerServiceWorld.com asked its subscribers, "Are You Ready for mService?"—the mobile evolution. Using Fred Newell and

Katherine Newell Lemon's new book, *Wireless Rules,*
eCustomerServiceWorld.com invited readers to test their knowledge of the future of wireless communication. You can take the
same quiz in our sidebar.

Fred Newell's Quiz

Here's Fred Newell's quiz, as presented by eCustomerServiceWorld.com.
See how well you score:

1. By what year will the number of wireless connections to the 'Net outnumber the number of wired?
a) 2002
b) 2005
c) 2007

2. How many wireless devices will be in the hands of U.S. consumers by
the end of 2001?
a) 50 million
b) 100 million
c) 200 million

3. What proportion of the European population will be surfing the 'Net
from their cell phones by 2003?
a) 10%
b) 20%
c) 30%

4. In five years' time, Japan will have more wireless phones than
a) Pets
b) People
c) Cars

5. By 2003, what share of Internet users will trust wireless transactions?
a) 22%
b) 43%
c) 63%
d) 83%

Answers
1. a) Wireless connections will outnumber wired by 2002.
2. c) 200 million wireless devices will be in the hands of U.S. consumers
by end 2001.
3. c) 30% of Europe's population will surf from cell phones by 2003.
4. b) People!
5. c) 63% of 'Net users will trust wireless transactions by 2003.

Manager's Checklist for Chapter 8

❏ Being present on the Information Superhighway is a none-gotiable if you want to maximize your CRM success—no matter what your business. Nearly half of all Americans buy online. Can you really afford not to be on the 'Net?

❏ The Internet can enable your customer relationship man-agement strategy to get information out to customers (Level 1), get information back from customers (Level 2), and complete e-commerce sales (Level 3).

❏ Information about you and your organization is out there on the Web, whether you planned it or not, whether you like it or not. It just makes sense to know and manage what's there.

❏ Use the Internet to learn about your customers and to give them opportunities to express concerns, ideas, and requests to you.

❏ Sales come immediately to mind when we think of e-com-merce. Make sure your e-commerce sales connections leverage your Customer Service/Sales Profile.

Managing Relationships Through Conflict

It's the nature of relationships to have conflict. Even the best relationships go through times of conflict. Just ask anyone who's been married or had a close friend longer than a few months.

With customers, conflict can come when you err, they err, some third party gets involved and errs, or even as a result of an act of God. Any time what you want as a customer is different from what you get, there can be conflict. Sometimes, there can be conflict when you get exactly what you asked for, but not what you expected.

Conflict can be destructive. And conflict can be constructive. Carol Kerr and her husband once spent a New Year's holiday at the historic Gallatin Gateway Inn in the mountains of western Montana. The entire stay had been wonderful until New Year's Day. They woke up late and padded down in their slippers for brunch expecting to find another exceptional meal awaiting them. To their dismay, they found the dining room was closed to refinish the floors. No one had mentioned this in any of the conversations they'd had with the staff in the previous four days of their stay. Fortunately Diane, who was working the front desk, remembered that the chef was staying at the Inn (having worked late on New Year's Eve) and called his room. Within minutes she had seated them in front of the fireplace in the bar, she had brought them mimosas, and she had the chef preparing a special meal just for them. Diane could've made the appropriate apologies and recommended a nice restaurant in town and made the conflict go away. But she intuitively saw the opportunity in the situation and created two very loyal customers who recommend the Gallatin Gateway Inn every opportunity they get.

In our experience, we miss the constructive opportunity when we go into conflict avoidance.

As a manager, your job is to remove fear of conflict. Give your employees the tools they need and an environment that encourages them to look for not only the response that makes the conflict go away, but also the opportunity to move the customer relationship to the next level of commitment.

Remember: "Problems are opportunities" becomes an empty platitude the first time you get angry or upset when an employee alerts you to a problem.

Nonverbal Signals Can Cause Problems

Michelle was a manager at a large travel agency in Denver, CO. She knew customer conflicts were important and, when told of them, immediately began to consider the best possible response. What Michelle didn't realize was that her "I'm thinking seriously" face looked a lot like many people's "I'm really mad at you" face. Her staff became fearful of bringing problems to her. It was during a 180-degree feedback session that Michelle learned that her nonverbal message was totally erasing her "Tell me about problems, I want to hear and help" verbal message. Today, Michelle tells this story to all her employees, so they know that the facial expression is just that—and she works at making her nonverbal message support her intention.

Managing the Moment of Conflict

It would be great to be able to identify and respond to potential conflict before it ever reached the level that the customer became aware of it. However, it's more often the case that a customer experiencing a problem or perceiving that a conflict exists brings it to our attention. In that moment, whether face to face, phone to phone, or over the Internet, there's an opportunity to save that customer relationship, as well as to identify other customers who may be at risk of disappointment. All too often, companies miss one or both of those opportunities.

Managing the moment of the interaction with the customer requires that everyone in your organization be clear about four things:

1. Each and every customer relationship is valuable.
2. Fixing or responding to the immediate situation is the first order of business.
3. Finding root causes is the second order of business (so you can prevent it from ever happening again).
4. One incident may be a bellwether, signaling you that other customer relationships are at risk.

Complaints: Listen Carefully

Kristin Anderson recently tried to make an early morning deposit at the ATM just outside her bank. The machine whirred and hummed, but couldn't pull the deposit envelope inside. It sounded like a mechanical problem, so Kristin hit the cancel button and left with her envelope. Later that morning, she went into the bank to make her deposit with a teller. She explained the ATM problem. "Well, it must be working now," he said, "because no one's complained." Oh yes, someone had complained—and was complaining right now! Because the teller didn't know (a) how important it is to value complaints or (b) how and to whom to report the complaint, he missed an opportunity to value this customer's willingness to report a problem and try again, and he missed an opportunity to save other customers from frustrating deposit attempts.

Do your staff members know the importance of managing every customer complaint?

Look for Problems

As managers, especially managers concerned with customer relationship management, it's incumbent upon us to actively seek out problems.

Value the Customer

When a customer service representative, or any employee, gets into task mode, it can be easy to forget to value each customer relationship and instead focus on the task at hand. Consider the cashier who patiently waits for a customer to dig the last needed penny out of wallet or purse, while a "Take a penny/Leave a penny" container sits on the counter within fingertips' reach. How many of your employees would be aware and take the initiative to tell the customer, "That's OK. I have the penny you need right here"?

Before you get too hard on your staff, it's important to realize that your own systems may be contributing to this lack of focus on the value of a customer. For example, to combat the continuing issue of employee theft, the cash drawer has to balance to the penny or there will be consequences. However, if the cashier and the team who put the cash register systems in place knew the

The Real Value of Your Customers

Use this simple formula:
Average value of a customer transaction: _____ × Number of transactions per year: _____ = Annual value of a customer × Number of years a customer is loyal: _____ = Lifetime value of a customer: _____.

real value of their customers, donating 10, 25, or even 100 pennies a day to the "Take a penny/Leave a penny" container would look like a great investment.

Fix the Immediate Problem First

The customer who's standing in front of you, who's on the phone with you, or who's just sent you e-mail must be the first order of business. Seminal research by e-satisfy.com and the U.S. Office of Consumer Affairs shows that most businesses hear from only 4% of unhappy customers. The other 96% of those unhappy folks just keep quiet—and the vast majority of them will just never do business with that company again. So, the customer who tells you about the problem is doing you a huge favor and deserves your utmost attention.

In addition, if you respond to a complaining customer with care and concern, it's possible to create a stronger relationship than you had before the conflict. Why? Because when everything is going along smoothly, customers may take you for granted. When they venture a complaint and are treated with appreciation and concern, they can really experience and value a relationship with you.

Our friend Susan purchased a Fiskars Kangaroo™ Container to hold the 40-gallon plastic bag while she removed the leaves from her yard. She discovered, however, that the overstuffed bag of leaves created a vacuum when she tried to pull it from the container. An innovative person, Susan solved the problem by poking some air holes in the bottom of the container. On a whim, she found the Fiskars Web site and sent an e-mail outlining the problem and her solution. The next day she received a personal reply acknowledging the problem and thanking her for her suggestion. She's

---

Put a Price on Their Heads

At Stew Leonard's Dairy Store in Norwalk, CT, employees are invited to envision customers with the figure $50,000 tattooed on their foreheads. At Stew Leonard's they estimate that the average customer will spend at least that much money during their lifetime of visits—and they want every employee to remember that.

Don't Mess Up to Make Up

Responding to a customer problem with care and concern can create a stronger customer relationship than you had before, just as the glue in a repair can make that part of the object stronger than it was before.

However, don't create conflict just to get an opportunity to apply some relationship glue. Most customer upsets are never brought to your attention. And oft-broken customer relationships, like oft-broken vases, lose much of their value.

eagerly waiting to see if new Kangaroo™ Containers will include her adaptation, but even if they don't, she now holds a warm place in her gardener heart for Fiskars.

Find the Root Cause After You Solve the Situation

The Japanese have a saying, "Fix the problem, not the blame." In American society, it sometimes seems that we are interested only in fixing the blame—and in making sure that none of it finds its way to us.

But it's important in customer relationship management to find the causes of customer conflict, not so that someone or some department can take the heat, but rather so together we can eliminate, or at least control, the incidence of the conflict. To do this, your CRM system should:

- Track complaints by type and frequency.
- Compare reported timelines and experiences with the actual facts.

For example, a large warehouse-type retailer we worked with received complaints from customers that "There's no one here to help me. I can never find anyone." Yet the staffing formula said that there was the "right" number of people on the floor for the volume of customers. Did the owner need

---

TRICKS OF THE TRADE   **Put Yourself in Your Customer's Shoes**

We've been working with a new resort where one of the featured activities is hiking. On one of our visits to the resort, we took a hike with one of the staff, Audie. Several hours later, we returned to the lodge tired and hungry after getting lost repeatedly while trying to navigate the trails. Recounting our adventures to the assistant manager, Audie remarked, "You know, I always thought customers were just stupid when they complained about our maps and trails being hard to follow. Now I understand why they have such a hard time finding their way!"

Sometimes the best way to find the root cause of a problem is to experience your product or service as the customer would. Take your map in hand and go hike the trail yourself! Make sure putting yourself in your customer's shoes is part of your CRM strategy.

An Ounce of Prevention ...

Kristin Anderson conducted a customer service assessment for a small community hospital. It was founded by a religious order and had recently been purchased by a large, secular healthcare chain. As part of the conversion, almost all of the religious icons were removed. But the nails and shadows on the walls remained. Kristin heard several visitors comment, "It looks like thieves broke in and stole everything." With all those shadows showing on the walls, it didn't make members of the community feel that the heritage of their hospital, of their community was valued. When the management team realized the problem, it didn't take long to pull all the nails, patch the holes, and put a fresh coat of paint on the walls.

Don't wait for a consultant to come in and point out the obvious. By the time several customers experience it, we guarantee that at least one employee is also aware. Use your CRM strategy to focus attention on resolving the conflict for good.

to bite the bullet of labor costs and add more staff to keep his customer relationships strong? No. Further investigation showed that the service representatives on the floor just weren't obvious to customers. A change in uniform to a bright vest changed the customer experience.

Identify and Nurture Other "At-Risk" Customers

One customer complaint or incident can be a signal that other customer relationships are at risk. Product recalls are a classic example of this principle.

The unfortunate, and sometimes even tragic, experience of one customer or a group of customers triggers the company to contact all customers, asking them to return the product or giving them the parts needed to make a safety adjustment.

Answer Simply a reply or response to a question or issue. The dictionary defines it in part as "A spoken or written reply or response to a question, request, accusation, or communication."

Solution Goes to the next level. The dictionary defines it as "The act of solving a problem." In other words, answers get customers off the line. Solutions build customer relationships.

Fix It Immediately and Fix It Right

Carol Kerr recently received an e-mail attempting to sell her on a "new, innovative, must-have product for trainers!" She wasn't interested, and was a bit annoyed that the e-mail began, "As a member of the _____ association, I know that you'll be interested in ...." So much for the association's promise not to sell her name. Not six hours later, Carol received an e-mail from the Member Services Director for the association. The message acknowledged and apologized for the unauthorized use of the association's e-mail list, thanked the members who had alerted the main office, and outlined the process for preventing such abuses in the future.

The earlier you can identify the cause of other at-risk customers, the less it will cost you—in direct expenses and in lost customer good will—to resolve the conflict for them, too.

Whether the conflict is large or small, physical or symbolic, reaching out to all affected customers tells them that you value their business and that you are actively nurturing your relationship with them. You aren't just providing quick answers to customer queries. You're providing real solutions that add value to the time, and money, they spend with you.

"But 'Nice' Never Bought Me a Customer"

"We already provide great customer service," the general manager enthusiastically explained. "I hardly ever hear a customer complaint. Oh, some customers are harder to deal with than others, but that's just the nature of people. The issue we face is price competition. 'Nice' never bought me a customer, but I've gotten plenty of them to switch vendors for a fraction of a cent. In our business (paper grocery bags), there is no such thing as customer loyalty." And, he implied, no real customer relationships to be managed.

We talked more with this general manager about his industry, his target customers, their buying patterns, and what he knew about his competition. Yes, you could find the evidence to build a strong case for price-focused competition. Customers did indeed switch for a fraction of a cent. But this analysis

Where There's a Customer, There's a Relationship

Is it possible that in some industries, in some sales situations, there isn't a real customer relationship to manage—in good times, much less in times of conflict? Yes, it can be true for *some* products and for *some* customers. Gasoline is a case in point.

Just look how far people will drive to save a penny on a gallon of gasoline. But even then, price isn't the only or even the dominant decision driver for all customers. For example, when two or more stations compete at a single intersection, claims of quality ("Fresher gasoline," one chain boasts about its prehistoric product) and service ("We provide full service at self-service prices") can be the distinguishers. And, while working with a national service station chain, we learned that successful stations have a core of loyal customers who place their relationship with the station over a penny in price.

So, if price appears as a key driver for your customers, don't be lulled into complacency, thinking that managing the customer relationship doesn't count. It does! And, in such a setting, CRM strategies and tools for managing relationships through conflict are even more important.

begged a critical question: how and why did price become the primary driver of the buying decision? This is a critical question because it's difficult, extremely difficult, to compete solely on price and make a profit.

Price becomes the critical driver when one of three situations exists:

1. Service quality seems *indistinguishable*—customers don't perceive any real difference between your offering and that of your competition.
2. Service quality seems *universally poor*—customers do not believe that any provider can be relied upon to provide a superior service experience.
3. Service quality seems *universally good*—customers believe they will receive an acceptable or even superior service experience at any location. This is more often true across a brand, such as a particular hotel chain, than across an entire industry segment.

In all three of these situations, the ability to identify, track, and respond to a conflict situation with ease and elegance can give you and your organization a marketplace advantage. You see, it's when things go wrong that you get the customer's emotional attention. Hold it carefully, value it, and soothe it into trust and exceeded expectations and you can win the customer's loyalty—a loyalty that is stronger than "a fraction of a cent." Let's look at what that means for each situation.

When Service Quality Seems Indistinguishable

Miller-Little Giant makes a very fine black rubber bucket for use on ranches and farms. The DuraFlex Pail is a great product, sold side by side with competing buckets, some of which may sell for less. "Crack-proof, crush-proof, and freeze-proof" proclaims the label. Sure, but who trusts a label? The proof comes when Daisy the cow steps on the DuraFlex and, behold, it isn't crushed. Miller-Little Giant tested its product to ensure that it could stand up to any farmyard incident. But, in the real world, customers are incredibly creative in their product use and abuse. What survives an angry cow may not last through an encounter with 10-ton truck. And when the worst happens, when against all odds the "crush-proof" is crushed, Miller-Little Giant wants to know about it. And—this is key—the company wants to make it right with the customer. So, Miller-Little Giant's sales force is in frequent communication with its dealer network. Or, Daisy's owner can tell Miller-Little Giant about the bucket disaster directly via phone or e-mail. It's Miller-Little Giant's prompt and caring response, focused on maintaining the relationship with the customer, that garners it superior loyalty in a market where there seem to be few distinguishers.

When Service Quality Seems Universally Poor

When an industry has a reputation for poor service, there is tremendous profit opportunity for any company that makes a strategic commitment to managing relationships through conflict. Few enterprises are as oft-maligned as the cable TV industry. Yet, before a larger company bought it out, Continental Cablevision of St. Paul, MN, was creating a very different reputation. It even won kudos from *TV Guide* magazine! How? By valuing and managing customer relationships, even in times of conflict.

While others in its sector had the attitude "If you don't like it, just try to be happy with a few measly broadcast stations," Continental Cablevision of St. Paul was finding ways to woo back unhappy customers. After analyzing why so many customers would discontinue their cable in the summer and then reconnect their service during the Thanksgiving marketing campaign, they created a plan to allow customers to put their cable "to sleep" for a month or three, while they spent the precious days of Minnesota's summer at the lake.

If a customer couldn't get the TV remote to work properly with the cable box, a service representative would call and visit via a special channel. While the conversation took place over the phone line, you—and any other interested customer—could watch the representative as he identified the exact make and model of your remote and then walked you through the

---

Turn Complaints into Service Opportunities

• List your five most common customer complaints.

• Analyze each complaint to find out the root cause. For example, Continental Cablevision of St. Paul noticed that many customers discontinued service in the summer and signed up again in the fall. Customer interviews revealed that customers resented paying for service in the summer while they weren't using it and were willing to go without service in September and October so they could sign up for free installation in November.

• Determine the cost of doing nothing. Is this a problem worth addressing? Continental Cablevision looked at both the lost revenue and the cost of removing each customer from its rolls and then adding that same customer back on four months later.

• Finally, determine the potential profit opportunity. Continental Cablevision found that a customer who might cancel for four months would often put his or her cable service "to sleep" for only two months, thus garnering two more months of revenue!

programming process until you reached success. One rep even took advantage of this service to show a customer a new cross-stitch technique. And customers loved it!

Continental Cablevision of St. Paul's success with its customers made it an attractive purchase. We hold out hope that others will try to copy its success; however, it doesn't appear that *TV Guide* will be giving more kudos to other cable providers any time soon.

When Service Quality Seems Universally Good

Here it helps to consider how customers view the reputation of companies, chains, and franchisers with a single brand who do business with their customers in many different locations.

For example, the Marriott Hotels are consistently ranked in the top echelon of guest satisfaction. A recent study by J.D. Power and Associates and *Frequent Flyer* magazine ranked Marriott third (in a tie with Hyatt). *Consumer Reports* affirms that, regardless of which Marriott property you visit, you can expect a clean, well-appointed room and a quality experience.

Marriott pays attention to customer relationship management. Through its awards programs, Marriott collects preference information and tracks usage. Marriott also encourages guests to give comments, good and bad, about their experiences, along with suggestions for improving. In addition, Marriott, like other high-quality hotel chains, tracks service performance by property. A guest complaint at a single property can harm the entire Marriott brand. Marriott's customer relationship management strategy recognizes that the value of a guest is far more than a single room for a single night. A guest is worth the sum total of his or her lifetime visits and the value of the other guests he or she will influence to also stay at Marriott—or to stay away. Conflict, whatever its cause, is a test of the consistency of the Marriott experience.

We shared information of the type we've just been describing with the general manager of the grocery bag company. "Oh, I see," he replied. "In our industry, customers expect plenty of conflict. And they don't believe any one provider is really better.

> ## Be Prepared for Conflict
>
> Half of all small businesses fail after one year, but only 5% of franchises fail. After five years, independent small businesses fare even worse, with 80% failing, while only 25% of franchises fail. Why?
>
> Michael Gerber, author of *The E Myth Revisited* (HarperBusiness, 1995), explains that a guiding principle for franchises is to create a consistent, predictable experience for their customers in all their locations. This includes creating a consistent, predictable, *and positive* experience when conflict occurs. Embrace this principle in your CRM strategy and make sure that your CRM tools support it.

Whether they buy from my competitor or me, they expect that they'll get a decent grocery bag delivered more or less on the date promised in more or less the quantity ordered with paperwork that is more or less correct. If they get a pallet where the printing is smeared, they'll send it back or even just use it, figuring that's the best they can expect. I *know* we do a better job than the other guy; a misprinted pallet wouldn't make it out of our factory. But we aren't doing anything to make our customers aware of that."

As our conversation continued, he began to see how, with a CRM strategy in place, he could begin turning the customer transactional data that already existed in various back-office systems into a valuable tool for creating customer loyalty.

Customer Relationship Management Is an Early Warning System

Every Tuesday morning, like clockwork, the management team at Acme Manufacturing met for a weekly update. Acme made and sold high-end exercise equipment, built-to-order units that were all the rage because of Acme's patented system. At each meeting, area managers reported the number of units built that week, the number shipped, and the number returned. They reported the financials and predicted future earnings. And they patted themselves on the back and said, "Good job" to each other while they silently thanked their stars that they were part of a "sure thing."

This day, however, the call center manager was late to the meeting. Very late. When she entered the room, her peers could see that something was wrong. "We've got a problem," she began. It seemed that for several weeks now, customer care representatives had been getting a few calls from customers asking where their merchandise was. Customers explained that the payment had been charged to their credit card and they had waited the six to eight weeks they were told to wait—or even longer. Now they wanted to know exactly when their exercise equipment would arrive.

When the reps tried to pull up the orders in their system, they could find no indication that the order had ever been sent on to manufacturing. The best they could do was reenter the order and tell the customer to wait another six to eight weeks. So, that's exactly what they did.

Talking with each other during breaks, the reps realized that more and more customers were calling with this same problem—and those customers were less and less understanding about the additional delay. They asked their manager about it. She said she would investigate and began running data reports. It took a day or two for the information technology group to link the payment report with the manufacturing report, but they did it.

"It's a big problem," the call center manager continued. "It seems that there was a system glitch with one of our sales channels," she explained. They were putting together a solution that would be implemented within 24 hours. But in the meantime, it would be a painstaking process to identify the missed orders, reenter them, and then inform the customers of the problem and the delay.

All customer relationships can go through times of conflict. Sometimes, like at Acme, conflict is caused when systems, technology, products, processes, or people fail. Customers can also be responsible for conflict. We're willing to bet that there isn't a person out there, including us, who hasn't at least contributed to a product or service problem. At other times, conflict arises because what customers want and what you provide no longer

Plan for Problems

Smart Managing

The senior management team at Schwan's Ice Cream, a family-owned company located in Marshall, Minnesota, holds monthly "Preventative Law" meetings. The meetings are named for the premise that the very act of planning for problems makes that problem less likely to occur—as we all know, popular belief says it's far less likely to rain if you have an umbrella with you. The Preventative Law group asks what kinds of problems or conflicts might rain down on Schwan's. For each problem, an umbrella plan is created for the first 24-48 hours of response.

Ask the same question about your customer relationships. Then, look at your CRM strategy and the tools that support it. What data reports could tell you that a storm might be brewing or that the rain is already here? Acme could have tracked customer problems by type. Any problem that happened to X number of customers could have triggered an alarm and an investigation.

match. Whatever the issue, your CRM strategy—the vision that drives it and the tools and technologies that support it—must stand ready to identify conflict early in the game and to help you recover customer trust and customer loyalty.

What happened at Acme Manufacturing can happen to any company whose CRM strategy and system are not poised to identify problems and support you and your team in handling

Create a Team of Trend Watchers

TOOLS

Acme's customer service representatives dealt with the "no shipment" problem for a long while before they raised the issue with their manager. Why? They didn't know what they were seeing. Turn your team into savvy trend watchers:

1. Include information about problem reports in your regular team meetings.
2. Ask staff, *frequently*, what types of comments and questions they've been hearing from customers.
3. Provide an avenue for your team to volunteer this information *before* you ask. You might have an online or paper form, or something as simple as your own open door policy.
4. Positively reinforce staff members for *all* the information they share with you—the false alarms and the real rain.

Anticipate Customer Needs

A managed healthcare provider tracked the number, reason, and length of calls made by enrollees in their first months of service. They found that customers frequently lost, misplaced, or simply never bothered to read their new member packets. It was easier, those customers felt, just to make a phone call. Easier for them—and more expensive for the plan.

Based on this customer intelligence, the service group began to make "welcome to our plan" calls to new enrollees. During the call they confirmed that the new member had received and could find the information packet. And they answered the top five new enrollee questions, before the enrollee had to call to ask. The result: happier and more cooperative customers and lowered expenses.

them. Of course we changed the name and some of the details, but the situation is true. And it's chilling to note that when Acme's patent expired, so too did its "sure thing."

What if the Customer Is the Problem?

The general manager at the bag company we spoke with said it: "Some customers are harder to deal with than others." Should your CRM system flag "difficult" (a.k.a. "eccentric," "demanding," "deadbeat," or even "outright mean") customers? The answer is yes ... and no.

We readily acknowledge that customers create a healthy portion of the conflict they experience. However, more often than not, as the service and product provider, you have an opportunity to mitigate or even eliminate that conflict experience. Noting and profiling customers who misuse or misunderstand your products and services can help you find better ways to do business with them.

The danger of flagging difficult customers as "difficult" is that it implies hopelessness about improving the quality of the customer relationship. The general manager we spoke with began our conversation so convinced that his customers were "price pirates," always seeking bounty at the manufacturer's expense, he couldn't see the opportunities for creating loyalty through customer relationship management that were there for the taking. Don't let flags on customer accounts or files create the same blind spot in your organization.

Manager's Checklist for Chapter 9

❑ Conflict is unavoidable. Don't be fatalistic, but accept the reality that you will indeed experience conflict in your customer relationships. At some point, for some reason, what I get as a customer isn't going to match what I expected.

❑ Make sure all your employees believe you when you say, "Problems are opportunities." Strategize ways to utilize CRM tools and process to make certain that conflict is a constructive experience that can help your business grow.

❑ At the moment conflict becomes apparent, your primary focus must always be fixing the immediate situation. First, make sure your CRM tools allow your employees to focus on the current customer and situation. Then look for ways to use your CRM tools and processes to identify root causes and opportunities to nurture other at-risk customers.

❑ If price appears to be the primary driver for your customers, effective strategies and tools for managing customer relationships through conflict can create a differentiator that puts you ahead of the competition.

❑ As you develop your CRM strategy, look for opportunities to build in early warning systems. Don't be blind-sided by problems that have already alienated many of your customers.

❑ As difficult as it is, always look for the silver lining in those difficult customers. What can they tell you that helps you further your relationship with all your customers—both the ones you have today and the ones you plan to have down the road?

Fighting Complacency: The "Seven-Year Itch" in Customer Relationships

The scene was a focus group interview with sales representatives. These men—and they were all men—sold high-tech, back-office solutions for financial institutions. Contracts were large and often negotiated for terms of five to seven years.

"What might make a customer choose to go with another vendor instead of you, when the current contract runs out?" the moderator asked.

"I'd have to be hit by a car, somehow not on the scene, because they loooooove me," replied one. The others laughed and nodded their heads.

"My customers are loyal to me," explained another. "I'm their knight in shining armor. Something goes wrong, they call me and I get it fixed."

"Smug" begins to describe the attitude in the room. It sounded like business was good, even great. With all those loyal customers, why was a consultant called in and taking up valuable selling time conducting focus groups? Because a large number of those supposedly very loyal customers had left, were thinking about leaving, were already talking with the competition.

There was a real and dangerous disconnect between how these sales professionals viewed the customer relationship and what actual customer buying behavior showed. Why didn't the sales team see it? And how can customer relationship management help you prevent it, whatever team you're on?

But They Love Me!

The sales reps in the focus group pointed to the most recent customer satisfaction survey as evidence of their strong bond with their customers. Many customers had included glowing remarks about their sales representative. The verbatim comments from those customers confirmed that there was a sincere and heartfelt belief that the sales representatives cared and worked hard on the customers' behalf. Yet, those results didn't explain the trend in contract renewal, or lack thereof.

The group had theories: "It's the economy. What can you do?" "It's all these mergers and acquisitions. They want to stay with me—with us—but they just can't because they have to go with the new owner's vendor." "I'm doing everything I can. It's those product developers that are to blame. I'm working on the relationship, but they aren't delivering on the product." Every theory contained some truth—the economy, the buyouts, "vaporware" products. But, even more important, every single theory let the sales representatives off the hook. What more could they do?

Ask the Right Questions

Customer satisfaction surveys only give you answers to the questions you ask. Review the survey you use. What is missing? What questions aren't you asking? Here are two key questions that should be included:

- Would you recommend Acme products and services? Why or why not?
- Have you recommended Acme products and services within the last three months? Why or why not?

Customers who say that they are satisfied or very satisfied with you, but who aren't motivated to recommend you, are relationships at risk.

This company had fallen under the allure of complacency. In the context of CRM, complacency is the self-satisfied, taking-it-for-granted belief that your customers are *your* customers. It's believing that because you've done the hard work of listening and learning, you now know them, they love you, and so the rest will be cake.

The Illusion of Complacency

The movie, *The Seven Year Itch*, rests on the premise that complacency is an illusion. George Axelrod's delightful farce shows that even a sensible man with a good marriage will begin to yearn for what he doesn't have. While his wife is at the seashore in Maine, Richard Sherman (Tom Ewell) sees his daydreams begin to take form with his new neighbor, Marilyn Monroe. It's a pleasant fantasy—until he realizes that his wife Helen (Evelyn Keyes) may have yearnings of her own. In the end, complacent no more, Richard rushes off to Maine to shore up the most important relationship in his life.

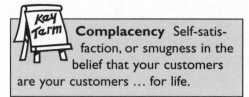

Complacency Self-satisfaction, or smugness in the belief that your customers are your customers ... for life.

All of us, and especially the sales representatives in our focus group, can learn three lessons from Richard Sherman's experience.

- Lesson 1: Everyone looks.
- Lesson 2: Don't expect them to let on that they're looking.
- Lesson 3: If you don't take actions to keep them, they may well wander.

When you understand these lessons, you can use the power of customer relationship management to keep your customers as *your customers*. And you can even expand those relationships and encourage customers to use more of your products and services, to actively seek new ways to be in partnership with you, and to recommend you to potential new customers.

Lesson 1: Everyone Looks

Everyone looks. Who do they look at? Your customers look at your direct competition. Sometimes they look with intent to shop. Other times with just a passing "Oh, there's anoth-er company offering those particular products and services." Whether or not they are seeking a new relationship, the fact that your customers are aware that the universe contains other possibilities impacts the way they view and relate to you.

The sales representa-tives in our focus group resisted this truth. They

> **Competing with Fantasy**
>
> **Smart Managing**
>
> Sure, your competitors aren't as alluring as Marilyn Monroe. You may believe, or even know, that they can't provide your level of quality. But does your customer know that? Really, really know that? Sometimes your harshest competition is when your customer gets the *idea*, the fanta-sy, that there is a better customer service partner out there, somewhere.

seemed to say, "Yeah, the competition is out there, but my cus-tomers, my very loyal customers, would never ever look unless they were *forced* to." In truth, their customers could not *not* look. (Just try to not notice your competition for a day.) What this lesson tells us is that we must always—before, during, and after the sale—consciously position what we offer vis-à-vis our competition.

Even if your direct competition isn't highly visible, your cus-tomers are always looking at and comparing the elements of the way you manage their service experience with the way simi-lar service experiences are managed by other service providers. Whether it is phone service, Web site access, billing, product packaging, the look of your facility, or any one of a myriad of other elements, your customers compare the experience they have with you and your team with the experiences they have with others. This is where CRM can be especially powerful in focusing all the parts of your organization on enhancing the customer relationship.

The Competition Is Always There

Help your team to avoid complacency by reminding them that competition is all around, always in sight. A great way to bring home this point is to illustrate that almost all of us have particular service providers to whom we are extremely loyal. Yet, at the same time as we espouse our loyalty we may, in fact, also do business with their competition. Ask your team: Do you have a favorite grocery store? Is it the only place you shop? Banks, dry cleaners, or online services can also provide great examples.

The point is that you are always competing for your customers' attention and business. Sometimes the competition is obvious, such as when you go head-to-head to win a contract. Subtler is the day-to-day competition that pits you and your organization against your customer's fantasy of ideal service.

Lesson 2: Don't Expect Them to Let on That They're Looking

A customer who is seriously searching for a new relationship may be very reluctant to let you know they are looking. That can be doubly true when they have a friendship with you or another employee, in addition to their customer relationship with your organization.

This was the case for the financial services company sales reps. Customers considering other options didn't want to hurt their sales rep by even suggesting that they might end the relationship. Yes, on occasion, a customer mentioned some frustrations and problems they were experiencing and the sales rep rode in like a white knight and got things straightened out. But the customer just couldn't get out the words, "We're glad you saved us. But we'd like to do business with a vendor who wouldn't put us in that position in the first place. And we'd like a sales rep who spent less time putting out fires and more time helping us build our success."

Lesson 3: If You Don't Take Actions to Keep Them, They May Well Wander

Whether they are actively looking or not, whether they tell you about it or not, it's up to you to reinforce the current relationship and to actively gather impressions, opinions, information, and experiences that will help you improve your offerings. This is what strengthens customer loyalty. And this is exactly what your CRM strategy and tools are poised to do.

In Chapter 1, we wrote, "With CRM, loyal customers aren't a happy accident created when an exceptional customer service representative, salesperson, or product developer intuits and responds to a customer need. Instead, you have at your finger-tips the ultimate advantage—customer intelligence: data turned into information and infor-mation turned into cus-tomer-satisfying action."

Looking is not neces-sarily about leaving. In fact, when customers review their alternatives, they often are more appre-ciative of what you offer. Carol Kerr tries to buy all of her grocery items at Central Market. The store is well lit, clean, attractive ... and large. Carol can

Pay Attention to Them All

The old adage is true: the squeaky wheel gets the grease. It's natural to pay attention to the cus-tomer in crisis or to the customer who is demanding. At such times, quiet, easy-to-serve customers often get taken for granted. Beware! The calm and cooperative customer may feel unimportant and unappreciated. Turn your back and that customer may walk away.

get most everything she needs, the very best-quality products, and all at a good price. Yet, Carol confesses that she also shops the competition when she's in a hurry because it's closer to home. And every time she does, she's left wondering, "Why can't they be more like Central Market?"

Your customers may not have the opportunity to comparison shop—and you may not want them that close to your competi-tion. In such cases, do it for them. Put what you offer into con-text by comparing and contrasting it with what else is out there.

The member companies of Contractors 2000 do an excellent job of this. In order to even be a member of Contractors 2000, a plumbing firm must be able to provide a superior level of service and quality. They must use only the best products and hire only highly qualified technicians. As a result, they are also not the low-cost providers of plumbing services. And under a "you get what you pay for" philosophy, that's actually a good thing.

Members understand that their relationship with the customer is made or broken not during the actual time of service, but rather when the customer talks to neighbors about they had done and how much they paid. Charlie Avoles, Executive Director for Contractors 2000, explains, "We want to come back to that house the next time plumbing services are needed, so before he or she leaves, a Contractors 2000 training technician makes sure the customer can explain what work was done, why it needed to be done, the advantages of having it done by one of our professionals, and why the price charged was fair and reasonable. It's a big job. Our [CRM] data on what customers ask about, call back about later, complain about and the like gave us the information we needed to put our explanations together."

TRICKS OF THE TRADE

Arm Them

Arm your customer to demonstrate the value of your relationship to a third party, whether a boss, spouse, friend, or sales professional from the other team Give your customer the words and information he or she needs to fully explain the value you offer.

An easy way to do this is to create a list of common customer questions and complaints. You may be able to pull them as a report from your CRM tool. Then ask your team to create answers—ideal responses to the customer—for each one. Review the answers together.

Customer Needs Change

Over time, what your customers need from you and how they want to do business with you will change. CRM provides a way for you to keep in touch with these changes, to even predict their direction and scope.

Kristin Anderson worked with the *Star Tribune* newspaper in Minneapolis some years ago, not long after an automated tele-

---

Change With Your Customers

Measure the pace of change for your customers. Create a
timeline for your company. Mark changes in what you offer
to customers and how customers do business with you. Whether your
timeline reaches back to the 1800s or just to the past 18 months, you
should see some significant shifts. If not, you may be caught in complacency—missing the changes that your customers want to make. Don't
let their last change be to a new service provider.

---

phone system for newspaper delivery "starts and stops" had
been installed. At that time, 20% of homes in the *Star Tribune*
delivery area had only pulse dialing and could not use the new
touch-tone system. Another, larger percentage of customers just
didn't want to talk to a machine. As subscribers began experiencing automated systems in other areas of their lives, the
process began to feel more familiar. When they realized that
they could now stop their morning paper before their trip out of
town, even when they didn't think about it until 11:30 p.m.,
many became strong advocates for it. Now, many of those
same customers are online.

Understanding the changing needs and desires of your customers is critical to continued success. If you don't understand
those changes, you lose your customers, little by little.

Don't Be Too Far Ahead

You may find yourself ahead of the curve of customer
change. Being ready with the next great thing before
your customers are ready to buy it can put you out of business. Or
make you a huge success.

Founded in Memphis, TN in 1916 by Clarence Saunders, Piggly Wiggly®
was America's first true self-service grocery store. Shoppers, accustomed
to presenting their orders to clerks, didn't know what to make of the self-
serve carts. But Saunders showed them how and the rest is history. (Read
more about it at www.piggly-wiggly.com/c_story.html.)
• Where are your customers leading you?
• Where are you leading the pack?
• Where could you be leading them?

Make Parting Such Sweet Sorrow

What if you spot a relationship where a customer is already on the way out, about to become a former customer? Don't give up. If the customer chooses to leave, it's also possible that the customer will also choose to return. The manner in which you handle things right now will be the last and most lasting memory for this customer.

The human temptation is to react to the news in one of two ways. On one end of the spectrum is giving up—"Oh, well, that customer is gone." So you turn your attention elsewhere. Yet, in the best case, the customer may not choose to leave after all.

The other end of the spectrum is to get angry—"Fine! We didn't want your business anyway." In fact, psychologists tell us that it's often easier for us to face a breakup when we are angry with the other person than when we feel rejected by him or her. And the same issue comes into play with customer service relationships.

To create the best possible parting, and even forestall it, follow these guidelines:

Reserve your value judgment. It may just be that you are no longer a good fit. No harm, no foul. Value judgments tend to force us into defending our positions. And defending often distracts from affirming what this customer really needed, what this customer really experienced during their relationship with you, and what this customer expects to experience with the new provider.

Conduct an exit interview. Using the channel of contact most preferred by this customer—be it phone, Web, or face to face—ask the customer to share with you any concerns or ideas. Ask why the customer is choosing to leave. And end the interview by telling the customer that you would welcome him or her to return at any time.

Share what you learn. Since no one department or area can have sole responsibility for CRM, use your tools to let others know what created the breakpoint for this relationship.

Renew Your Vows

Good friends of ours had a rather unusual marriage agreement. Every year, on New Year's Day, John and Susie renewed their wedding vows. "It's really a contract," Susie explained. "We want to remind ourselves every year of the promises we've made and of our commitment to follow through on them." In 1987, that sounded a little strange. In 2001, Dr. Phil McGraw is burning up the sales charts recommending similar ways to negotiate your relationship in his book, *Relationship Rescue: A Seven-Step Strategy for Reconnecting with Your Partner*.

Customer relationships also need periodic celebration and affirmation. And, after times of change, they also may need to be renegotiated. Use your CRM data to determine an appropriate time interval for your customers. In your situation, it may be every year or every three years or every three months.

Manager's Checklist for Chapter 10

❏ Remember: the questions you ask customers determine the answers they can give. Be sure to ask questions that enable customers to tell you what they're *really* thinking.

❏ Your CRM strategy should encompass understanding which customers are at risk, why they're at risk, market/industry trends, and where your customers are going. You want to be there with them!

❏ Even when customers leave, CRM doesn't stop. Departing customers are great sources of information that helps you keep other customers. Besides, parting on good terms and using the information they provide to improve your customer relationships greatly increases the likelihood that those departed customers will be back.

❏ Periodically "renew your vows" by reviewing expectations with your customers. It's not so much about the next contract as it is about understanding what you each need to be successful going forward and how you can continue to support each other's success.

Resetting Your CRM Strategy

N ow you are on the final chapter. You've created a strategy.
You've investigated specific topics like e-commerce and
handling conflict. And you've been reminded in Chapter 10 that,
to be successful, your CRM initiative needs to keep moving forward. What's left? Some how-to's for sustaining your CRM
effort. In this chapter we'll apply a process for assessing, align-
ing, and continually renewing your CRM strategy.

Michael Hockmuller, a senior organizational development consultant for the City of Austin, TX, calls this process "conducting a
corporate reset." As Michael explains, "We created this process as
a check for our business plans, and find it works well for testing
any organizational strategy. The purpose is to find alignment
between what customers want, what our strategy tells us to do,
and the tactics we've chosen to implement that strategy. Sometimes we are right on track, but usually one of two things has
happened. Either customer needs have shifted, so our strategy no
longer points us in the best direction. Or, there has been 'drift' in
what employees are doing to implement the strategy. A corporate
reset ensures that everyone is implementing the right strategy for
the right reasons." We've customized this process for use in resetting your CRM Strategy.

> **Follow Through**   TRICKS OF THE TRADE
>
> Most managers and executives begin strategy development with
> positive intentions about revisiting the process, renewing goals, and
> making adjustments to reflect market changes. Yet, in the hectic activities
> of day-to-day operations, those good intentions can fall to the wayside.
> To help you follow through:
> - Set a date in your planner today for your first and second—and
>   even third—CRM strategy reset. Make a written commitment to
>   yourself to follow through.
> - Include resetting your CRM strategy as one of your annual objectives.
>   Make a commitment to your boss, and ask to be held accountable.

Ready, Set, Reset!

The process for resetting your CRM strategy has three phases.
As in Chapter 4, where we looked at a process for creating your
CRM strategy, the way that you implement this process will vary
with the nature and complexity of your customer relationships.
However, the basic roadmap remains the same. Phase 1 looks
at how your CRM strategy is impacting your target customers.
Is it working to create the experiences, the buying patterns, the
recommendations, and the expanded business opportunities
you originally sought to create? Phase 2 requires you to look
internally. How well is your CRM strategy understood, received,
and implemented by the employees responsible for creating and
managing your customer relationships? In Phase 3 we take the
information learned by looking outward and inward and use it to
reset the CRM strategy.

Phase 1. Are You Hitting Your Target?

The ultimate test for your CRM strategy and the tactics you're
using to implement it is *customer satisfaction*. Go back to your
ideal Customer Service/Sales Profile. Are you getting the number
of initial/stand-alone transactions that you want or need to give
your profile a strong foundation? How about repeat customers?
And customer advocates? Are the percentages of each of the
three levels of customer relationship right for your business?

Smart Managing

Subjective and Objective

CRM measures can come in the form of *subjective* measures, such as customer satisfaction surveys or tracking complaints and compliments. And CRM measures can be *objective*, looking for hard data such as average length of transaction, transaction accuracy, ability to resolve customer issues in the first contact, and the like. Make sure you look at both.

There are at least four questions you need to ask in Phase 1 of your CRM strategy reset.

- *Are your CRM strategy measures in place?* You will typically have CRM measures at two levels. The first measure the overall CRM strategy and often look specifically at how well the CRM strategy contributes to the larger organizational business goals and objectives. The second measure the individual tactics you implement. For example, measures of customer retention or customer churn address overall business goals. Measures of length of time on hold or in line address tactics.

- *Is the data from your measures being collected, analyzed, and shared with the right people in your organization?* For example, comparing the two types of measures cited in the paragraph above can tell you which tactics contribute to your overall goals, which are neutral, and which may actually detract.

For Example

Knowing Enough

A call center manager who knows everything to know about average length of call but doesn't also know how that relates to customer satisfaction, customer loyalty and customer buying behaviors doesn't know enough.

- *Are the measures accurate?* Just because you have a system in place to capture CRM performance data, doesn't mean that that system is working.

- *Are your measures an appropriate reflection of your CRM strategy?* If, for example, your CRM strategy stresses creative and innovative solutions to customer problems and needs, that implies that you will value creative and inno-

vative employees.
However, an organi-
zation we're familiar
with tracked these
"creative and innova-
tive" solutions by
asking employees to
fill out "exception
reports" every time
they had to create a
special solution. The
tone of the measure-
ment and tracking
process made

Accurate Measures

Kristin Anderson recently
worked with a client to analyze customer transaction data for
trends in customer spending patterns.
She was the first to notice that,
depending on how you asked the POS
(Point of Sale) system to run the data,
you could get some very different
numbers. Not good—and, actually very
easily corrected—once the problem
was surfaced.

Are you using inaccurate or mis-
leading CRM performance measures?

employees feel defensive and a bit concerned that they
were going to get in trouble for working outside the
box. This is not the
way to encourage
creative responses to
customers.

Phase 2. Does Your
CRM Strategy Work
for Your People?

This phase is about checking in with the employees
responsible for creating,
managing, and expanding
customer relationships. Is
your CRM strategy working
for them? If they do not

**The Reluctant Yes
Problem**

Smart Managing

"I don't get as concerned
about hearing 'no' to one of these four
questions, as I do about failing to hear
a resounding 'yes,'" explains Steven
Dietz, an OD consultant with the City
of Austin, TX. "If I hear a 'no,' the problem is likely to be obvious to everyone, and it will be relatively easy to
focus attention on fixing it. It's the
qualified or reluctant 'yes' that can
allow poorly aligned strategies and tactics to remain in place."

feel aligned with your CRM strategy, it won't matter how carefully you crafted it, and it will never live up to its potential.

We find that internal focus groups are a terrific tool for this
phase. In a small department or functional area, you may
want—and be easily able to—involve all employees. For larger

Missing the Mark

Carol Kerr recently signed up to rent movies at a new video store. Completing the 6-inch by 4-inch new member form, she noticed that it asked for her home phone number and ZIP code twice. Why? "Because that's the way we have to enter it into the data base. They use one phone number to search for your record. The other is so we can contact you if there is a problem."

It's great that the technology system is designed to easily pull up customer records, but asking the customer to write—and the service representative to enter—the same number twice doesn't make sense. Can you find examples in your department or area of CRM tactics, tools, or measures that miss the mark?

areas or for a company-wide CRM strategy, look to talk with a representative sample of employees.

They're All Important

Smart Managing It's obvious to think about employees who have direct contact with your external or internal customers. Don't forget, however, to include the important employees who support them.

Create a discussion guide of the topics you wish to cover and the questions you will ask. Your discussion guide should also include:

• **Introductions.** Usually, you will ask someone outside your department, or even a professional focus group facilitator, to guide the discussion. The facilitator, often called the moderator, should introduce himself or herself and provide an opportunity for the participants to introduce themselves.

• **A statement of purpose.** Explain that you are working on resetting your CRM strategy and that their feedback is vital to the process.

• **A statement of confidentiality.** If you are recording the session, how will the audiotape be used? Usually, you will explain that the focus group report or summary will include participant comments, but that no participant will be identified by name.

> **Focus groups**   Guided discussion groups of six to ten partici-
> pants. The purpose is to elicit reactions, ideas, and concerns.
> (Note: Focus groups are not a time to correct or educate.)
>   There are many great books and resources for conducting focus
> groups. We still go back to Ron Zemke and Thomas Kramlinger's classic
> *Figuring Things Out: A Manager's Guide to Needs and Task Analysis* (Addison-
> Wesley, 1982) for a description of the employee focus group process.
>   Folks from your organization's market research area will tell you
> that there is a science, with very specific rules, for conducting focus
> groups. We often take a more relaxed approach with internal focus
> groups, but for the novice facilitator it makes sense to start more for-
> mally and to use someone with experience as your focus group dis-
> cussion leader.

- **Housekeeping about the process.** Tell the group how long
  the focus group will last. Plan for 90 minutes as an average length. You may want to ask participants to turn off
  pagers and cell phones.

Discussion questions for a CRM strategy reset may include:

- It's important for any business to create, maintain, and
  expand customer relationships. What approach or
  approaches does your department or functional area use
  to accomplish this? (The moderator may use a flip chart
  to capture a list of comments.)
- Do you believe (a particular approach) is working? Has
  it been helpful to you in your contacts with customers?
  Why or why not?
- What do you think your organization should do to create,
  maintain, and expand customer relationships?

One of the things that we often find is that support employees feel out of the loop when it comes to your CRM strategy.
They may be focused on their specific job tasks but often feel
disconnected about how and why their job duties are important
to the company and its ability to serve and retain customers.

Special Treatment for Special Customers

To avoid routine responses, employees in all areas must continually focus on being sensitive to customer needs, especially when those needs change and process or tactics are realigned to better meet them.

One research firm began to do a lot of government contract business. Government customers have some unique needs. As you might expect, there is a lot of paperwork and a number of hoops to jump through when you are a supplier to a government agency.

The account managers failed to explain these new customer requirements to employees in an internal support area. These employees began to see the government customers as being unreasonable and demanding. They resented the special treatment these customers required.

After this attitude surfaced through an employee opinion survey, management was able to take steps. They met with this group and began to give them the information they needed to understand why government customers needed to be handled differently, how important this new segment was to overall business goals, and why the CRM strategy supported all these extra efforts to please this customer.

The result? Support services were no longer at odds with front-line contact employees and their government customers. Service and satisfaction improved for everyone.

Phase 3. Time for Change

Now, you're ready to create the reset for your CRM strategy. Pull together the information you gathered in Phase 1 and Phase 2. It may be helpful to display your key findings in two parts.

First, list the CRM strengths and successes you uncovered. It's important to acknowledge and celebrate what you're doing well.

The second part of your key findings identifies weaknesses. Prioritize this list. If your findings show that you need a major CRM strategy reset, revisit Chapter 4 and use that process once again.

More often, your list of weakness or opportunities will focus on specific CRM tactics and tools. You can address these in a working session with a group of the individuals responsible for

> **Is It Strategy or Tactics?** ⚠️ CAUTION!
>
> In our experience, CRM strategies have more longevity than CRM tools and tactics. As you move into Phase 3, be cautious about information that seems to say that you need to totally redesign your CRM strategy. More likely, it is the tactics and tools you're using to implement it that are misaligned.
>
> We've seen more than one case where CRM databases and information collection tools hijacked the CRM strategy process. When tools drive the process, it's easy to get caught up in all the things you *could* do, or that customers *should* want, and to miss what they actually require and what works.

customer relationships. Again, use some of the brainstorming processes described in Chapter 4. And remember those Post-it™ notes we told you to keep—the ones that your team used to create your initial list of potential CRM strategies? Now is the time to pull them out, dust them off, and use them to jump-start your new discussions.

> **Don't Forget to Celebrate!**   Smart Managing
>
> Usher in your reset CRM strategy and newly realigned tactics with a celebration of your successes. This can be a terrific time to do an annual awards event for employees in your organization or department who've gone above and beyond for customers or who contributed to your CRM approach with their innovative ideas.

Closing Words

There are three final thoughts we would like to leave you with as we bring this book to a close.

Having a clear and appropriate CRM strategy is a nonnegotiable for business today. Your CRM strategy should link to and support the overall business strategy and goals for your organization. This is as true for internal service-providing functional areas, as it is for non-profit and volunteer organizations, as it is for government organizations, as it is for traditional consumer retailers. It doesn't matter who your customers are, what types of products and services you provide, or what forces are acting upon your marketplace. Every manager needs a CRM approach

Tool Test

Smart Managing   How do you know if you have the right CRM tools? Certainly not by choosing the biggest and newest, the one with the most bells and whistles.

The right CRM tool for you is the one that:
- Allows you to implement your CRM strategy
- Works for you (and you and your team are willing to work it)
- Works for your customers, and
- Is affordable.

as a guide to business success.

CRM is a comprehensive approach for creating, maintaining and expanding customer relationships. It's a mistake to confuse your CRM approach with the tools and tactics you choose to help you implement it. Your CRM tools may be high-tech or low-tech.

CRM tools can't substitute for good customer service skills. At the end of the day, the best customer experiences are human and feel humane. It takes people—people who understand what customers want and who care about delivering it to them—to create those experience. Even if the customer and the service provider never meet, when solid customer-handling skills inform the design of the e-commerce interaction, satisfaction is increased.

We'd love to hear what you are doing to create, maintain and expand customer relationships. If you have a comment, a question, or an idea to share, please let us know. You can contact us by:

E-mail: Kristin@KristinAnderson.com
Phone: 952 920-2628
Mail: Kristin Anderson and Carol Kerr
         Say What? Consulting
         3902 West 50th Street, Suite A
         Edina, MN 55424

Manager's Checklist for Chapter 11

❑ Conduct a CRM strategy reset to find alignment between what customers want and what your strategy tells you to do and the tactics you've chosen to implement that strategy.

❏ The ultimate test for your CRM strategy and the tactics you're using to implement it, is customer satisfaction.

❏ Resetting your CRM strategy has three phases: how your CRM strategy impacts target customers, how well your CRM strategy is understood, received and implemented by employees, and how to take what you learn to create the actual "reset."

❏ Having a clear CRM strategy is a non-negotiable.

❏ CRM is about your approach, not the size of your tools.

❏ CRM can't substitute for high quality customer service skills.

Index